A Prairie
Kitchen

A Prairie Kitchen

Recipes, poems and colorful stories
from the *Prairie Farmer* magazine, 1841-1900

Compiled by Rae Katherine Eighmey ● Published by Farm Progress Companies

Designed by Al Casciato
Edited by Linnea Schlobohm

Illustrations for this book have come from 1841 to 1888 editions
of *Prairie Farmer* magazine and other period sources.

Published by Farm Progress Companies
191 South Gary Avenue
Carol Stream, IL 60188
Telephone: (630) 690-5600
www.farmprogress.com

First Printing

0-9720552-0-7

This book is dedicated to those who lived in the Prairie Kitchens and is written for my children and grandchildren — Liz and John, Justin and Jack — who will enjoy and value reading about them.

ACKNOWLEDGEMENTS

This book could not have been written without the countless, and largely nameless, 19th-century contributors to *Prairie Farmer*. The identity of the editors, columnists and many of those who wrote letters and suggestions have been lost to time, but their recipes and suggestions are timeless in their value. I am grateful to have been able to read and interpret them.

In the 21st century, there are many who should be thanked as well. Folks on the interpretive staff at Living History Farms near Des Moines who presented the opportunity to concentrate my 19th-century food research on the Midwest. Frank Holdmeyer of *Wallaces Farmer* magazine, who thought this cookbook would be a good project. Sara Wyant at Farm Progress Companies, who gave me the go-ahead and moral support. Thank you to Rosemary Schimek for her good suggestions for the cover; to Al Casciato whose vision and design converted my manuscript into a beautiful book, and most especially to Linnea Schlobohm, dedicated and careful editor. Thank you. Your attention and cheerful suggestions have kept me from making too many mistakes in form and content. This book is much better for your contributions to it.

Finally a special thank you to my husband, John, who not only suggested I give Frank a call but who cheerfully, yet critically, ate many, many samples as I refined the recipes. I could not have done this project, or anything else, without you.

INTRODUCTION

I started cooking with old recipes more than twenty years ago after I opened my grandmother's 1920's recipe box and found it filled with wonderfully tempting batter-spattered cards. A couple of years later, during research for a historic house museum, a friend gave me two cookbooks from the 1860s, and I was hooked. I felt as though I had moved my kitchen back into the 19th century as I researched lifestyles, cooking equipment and ingredients, finding more and more recipes that demanded to be cooked.

Since then I've spent thousands of hours in bookstores, libraries and my kitchen once again creating the wonderful recipes that were part of the everyday life of our great-grandparents. I've used original issues of *Prairie Farmer* magazine for the past 15 years as a resource for 19th century recipes. But in developing this cookbook, I've grown in appreciation of the knowledge, humor, concerns and warmth contained in its pages. Dinner menus at our home are most often made up of these dishes common in prairie kitchens. These good foods, simply made, seem to give our guests a satisfaction of mind and spirit. It is an experience I hope the recipes and commentary in this book will enable you to share with your family and friends.

The 19th century issues of *Prairie Farmer* are totally engrossing. Countless hours disappeared as I scrolled through the microfilmed issues making selections for this book. I was witness to a lively printed "chat room" of suggestions, ideas, innovations, comments, criticisms and questions among subscribers in several Midwestern states. Letters came from towns in Indiana, Illinois, Wisconsin, Iowa, Nebraska and Kansas. In these pages, the struggles and successes of prairie pioneers came alive through the words of scores of individuals who shared their experiences with fellow readers. I read what it took to make successful prairie farms in the 1840s and 1850s. I looked forward, as the farm wives must have in the 1870s, to Clara Francis' weekly Housekeeping columns. I've come to know the ladies in the 1880s Housekeepers Improvement Club.

Since its first issue in January 1841, *Prairie Farmer* has been an invaluable resource for farmers, farm homemakers, grain and cattle traders, and merchants. Recognizing that those who came to settle the western prairies were encountering conditions and circumstances totally new, even to experienced farmers, the first editors set out to make this eight-page paper interesting and valuable.

If you wanted to learn how to "break the prairie" *Prairie Farmer* had articles telling you how. If you wondered what would make a good hedge, *Prairie Farmer* readers suggested a number of plants and even told you where to get seeds for the Osage Orange. If you needed cures for animal diseases, news of implement successes, current cattle and crop prices and, of course, recipes, *Prairie Farmer* was the place to turn.

The first editor put it this way in 1841: "No editorial skill can make it what the West demands, but if as soon as a farmer obtains one fact, he sends it, it will be what we want — short and sweet.'" Subscribers were urged to "sit down immediately and communicate" information of interest and value to other farmers. And fill the pages they did. Amid articles by the editors and columnists reporting on market activity and national trends are letters and pieces sent in from all over the Midwest.

Over the years, *Prairie Farmer* printed pieces that were straight to the point with blunt opinions on issues of domestic economy and agricultural success. Stories from the farm and Civil War battlefield filled the pages, along with international opinions and domestic innovations. Some were amusing and some profound; all were useful. The overriding goal of the magazine was to give prairie settlers as much information as possible to make their lives easier and their enterprises a success. That information is valuable today for anyone who wants to understand prairie life and our cultural roots and values.

Nowhere is this value more evident than in the household columns. In the earliest Household Department columns, a few basic recipes — corn bread, preserving hams, butter-

making and simple preserves — were scattered among more essential hints such as treating scours in calves, gapes in chickens and horn distemper.

In the late 1850s, the editors of *Prairie Farmer* began setting aside a column in each issue seeking an exchange of information "interesting to farmers' wives." The editors headed the column with this request: "Will not our lady readers contribute recipes, experiences in household management — indeed anything that will be interesting and valuable to farmers' wives — to this column. And if anything finds a place here, that is impractical, we shall be glad to receive criticism on, or corrections of the same. Practical household matter is wanted."

Throughout the Civil War era, the magazine continued to publish household information, although not in every issue. Space was given over to coverage of the War — news of Sherman's raid, enlistment requests and articles sent in

by farmers now turned soldiers. However, for a time in the middle of the 1860s, *Prairie Farmer* included household columns that were credited to Marie Mignonette. I don't know much about Marie. It seems as though she grew up on a farm, but her articles were written with "city poisoned ears." In her role as a columnist, she urged country cooks to continue to make healthful and hearty meals. Later some *Prairie Farmer* correspondents suggested that a person named Marie Mignonette had no business offering housekeeping advice to farm homemakers, but as you can see from her recipes I've included, such criticism was unfounded.

In the 1870s, the *Prairie Farmer* reflected the growing successes of Midwest agriculture. It expanded to 24 pages and the household column had a page of its own. Clara Francis wrote some of the best pieces during this decade. Her words are witty and give thoughtful perspectives on nutrition and general health. She also contributed many delightful recipes. Clara's lemon cream pie and ginger lemonade, included here, are both easy to make and delicious.

During the 1880s, the homemaking column apparently became too much for one woman to write. The editors formed the Housekeepers Improvement Club, which met every other week to discuss a topic of mutual interest. At the top of each week's column is an illustration of the ladies meeting around a dining room table. An accompanying editor's note encouraged reader participation. "Every lady reader of the *Prairie Farmer* is considered a corresponding member of the Club and is invited to send in any notes, descriptions, suggestions, inquiries, answers to questions, etc."

The secretary of the Club took notes, which then became the column. They gave suggestions for children's lunches, tasty dinners, the best way to preserve farm garden bounty and the like. The column expanded to more than a page and included needlework projects, both practical and fancy. The names of many women are given as members of the Housekeepers Improvement Club. I've used many of their quoted opinions. That said, I find myself wondering if there really was such a Club. Certainly readers sent in recipes and suggestions, but I am skeptical that a group of women met weekly. I suspect the Club was a clever editor's way of providing a variety of opinions on subjects of the day.

I found limiting my selections from the first 50 years of *Prairie Farmer* difficult. I tried to pick representative recipes and articles across the decades. In the process, I found several new favorite recipes: cucumber catsup, beef with lemon, cookies without eggs and pumpkin butter. I hope you will find your own favorites. I am certain you will come away from the time you spend with this book refreshed and inspired by the humor, energy and dedication of the people who helped settle the prairie.

CONTENTS

COOKING WITH THESE RECIPES

Most of the recipes have been rewritten with standard measurements and methods for the modern kitchen. Some of them have been left in original *Prairie Farmer* language. These are printed in *italic*. These unedited recipes provide insights into life in the prairie kitchen that are intriguing and sometimes amusing, such as the one for steak that calls for tenderizing the meat by "beating it with a rolling pin for 10 minutes."

ABOUT COOKING EQUIPMENT

In converting these recipes to modern use, I retained the factors critical to the flavor and texture of the dish, while taking advantage of modern equipment. Farm wives enjoyed having labor saving equipment and household gadgets. I am sure a 19th-century farm wife would have gladly used a food processor and even a microwave oven, so I see no reason not to take full advantage of them here. And even though I have used my food processor extensively, don't be concerned it you don't have one. You can certainly chop, slice, dice, and mix by hand or with other equipment.

The only items you might not own that are essential for making these recipes are a food mill, or fine sieve, and a flour sifter. I use an 8-inch sieve for sifting, straining sauces and pressing vegetables and fruits through to remove seeds and skins. Cheesecloth and lint-free cotton or linen (not terry cloth) dish towels are necessary for straining some of the mixtures.

Cooking and baking pan sizes are different too. I am still struggling with just how big a pie pan was during frontier days. One commonly used pan reference is to "gem pans." The closest equivalent we have is mini-muffin pans. Of course any bread or cake can be baked in any pan. The key is to allow enough room for the dough or batter to rise without running over. Also recognize that larger pan sizes frequently require longer cooking times and, sometimes, lower temperatures. And if you intend to store any of the pickles or relishes longer than the time noted or differently from the recipe's instructions, consult a home canning guide for the current processing requirements necessary to assure a healthful product.

ABOUT INGREDIENTS

Frequently pioneer recipes will suggest to "flavor as you like" or "flavor as usual." For cakes and cookies, this would not have been vanilla or chocolate. Rather, spices such as mace, nutmeg, allspice, cinnamon, and ginger were popular flavoring. For meat dishes, herbs such as summer savory, thyme, marjoram, and parsley were used as well as spices such as cloves, nutmeg and cinnamon.

The ingredient called "powdered" sugar in recipes from the 1860s or earlier refers to granulated white sugar. In the early part of the 19th century, white sugar was sold in solid cones. The housewife would snip off an appropriate amount with her sugar shears and "powder" it for use in recipes.

Saleratus, an early form of baking soda, was used for making cakes and cookies rise.

On the prairie, flour had different properties, depending on the kind of wheat, how it was milled, how long it had been in storage, and even if it had been purchased in town. In the last part of the 19th century, flour was sometimes "stretched" by the manufacturer with sawdust or other nonfood substances. All of these conditions affected baking results. Even today, flour today can vary in its properties. Some recipes for breads and cookies may take slightly more or less flour depending on the conditions of storage and freshness.

ABOUT MEASURING

In early prairie kitchens, measuring was frequently done with whatever was at hand. "Butter the size of an egg" is a commonly used reference. Tea cups and coffee cups were pressed into service, as well as whatever spoons were available. Later, we find references to farm wives using scales to measure ingredients by the ounce or pound. But in some cases, measurements were not

even used. "Add flour to make like pancake batter" is one such helpful direction. In other cases, obscure standard measures are used such as drachm and gill. I have developed my own translation through years of trial and error.

Butter the size of an egg = 1/3 cup
Tea cup = measuring cup
Coffee cup = 1 1/4 cups
Drachm = 1/8 teaspoon
Gill = 1/2 cup
Tablespoon (in early recipes, before 1870) = 1/4 cup
Teaspoon = standard measuring teaspoon

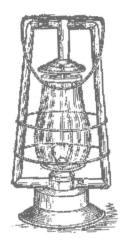

CHAPTER ONE

Breads

Corn bread was a mainstay of the frontier diet and forms the backbone of this chapter. The earliest version was "Journey cake" or what we have come to call "Johnny cake." This simplest unleavened mixture of corn meal and water, sometimes enriched with an egg, was baked on an oak board leaning up against the campfire.

"With good bread I am never worried if we are out of cake or pie." **Prairie Farmer, June 5, 1886**

Once the cabins were built, home-makers could begin to bake their corn bread on the hearth in a Dutch oven or spider, a frying pan with legs. Later, when wheat flour became a kitchen staple, *Prairie Farmer* writers included bread recipes that used both corn meal and wheat flour.

After the Civil War, it appears that corn breads fell out of favor. Few new recipes in the pages of *Prairie Farmer* featured corn meal. Rich tea cakes and muffins with fanciful names such as puffets, Sally Lunn or English buns were receiving all the attention.

By the 1880s, however, the food writers in the magazine once again recognized the value of using corn meal and the newer milled "graham" or whole-wheat flour for making hearty and healthful breads.

The way breads were raised changed during the first five decades of *Prairie Farmer*. Pioneer women would keep their own yeast starter, taking out a cup to make a batch of five or six loaves at a time, replenishing it and setting it aside to regain strength.

Many of the starter recipes begin with potato water with the addition of hops. Some period diaries suggest that, in the absence of hops or a previous starter, prairie settlers would leave the potato water uncovered, capturing naturally occurring yeast. The raising process is much longer using this type of yeast. A friend who tried this method made a very nice sourdough, but it took all day for the loaf to rise.

Even with a good starter, bread making was time consuming. Original recipes call for mixing the bread dough in the evening after the supper dishes are done and having the first rise overnight. Then the homemaker would form the loaves, light the kitchen fire, cook and serve breakfast. By that time, the loaves would have finished rising, and she was ready to bake her bread for the day. I have used instant rapid-rise yeast in these recipes with success.

Slap Jacks

1/2 cup corn meal
1 tablespoon flour
1 cup milk
1 egg

Mix the flour with the corn meal. Heat the milk to scalding. Stir in the corn meal and flour and set aside to cool. Beat the egg into the cooled corn meal. Preheat a griddle as for pancakes and lightly brush with butter. Put a scant tablespoon of batter on the griddle; turn when the edges are bubbly and the center looks dry. Serve hot with butter.

April 24, 1859
In ancient days the precept was, "Know thy self." In modern times, it has been supplanted by the far more fashionable maxim, "Know thy neighbor and everything about him."

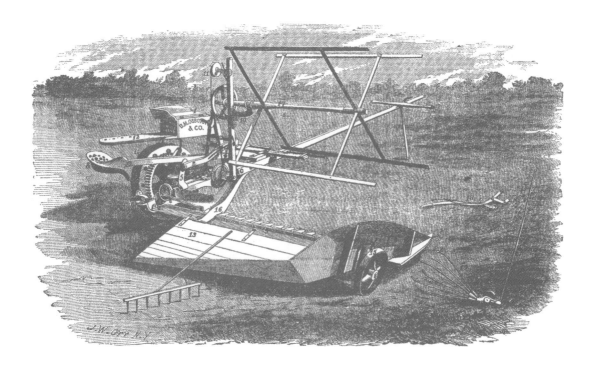

Corn Cakes

Editor's note:

These two early recipes (Slap Jacks and Corn Cakes) are examples of the important role corn meal served in prairie farm kitchens. Cookbooks intended for eastern or city dwellers did not have very many corn meal or corn bread recipes. Out on the developing prairie, however, corn meal was the staple. Some early prairie diarists write of having corn meal mush for days in a row as the only dish, with dried wild currants and honey to provide some variety.

Their secret to exceptional corn bread was to always swell the grains before mixing with the other ingredients. This gives the bread, or slap jacks, a much nicer texture by eliminating the "gritchieness" common in coarsely ground meal simply used as flour. You might try adapting your favorite corn bread recipe to that technique.

2 cups mush, almost cold
3 eggs, separated
1 cup milk
2 cups corn meal
1 1/2 tablespoons melted lard
1 large spoon butter on each cake

Preheat the oven to 350 degrees F. Make the corn meal mush by combining 2 cups of hot water with 1 cup of cornmeal. Stir until the grains are swollen and set aside to cool. Combine the egg yolks with the milk and stir into the mush. Add the corn meal and melted lard (or butter or margarine). Mix well. Whip the egg whites until stiff and fold into the batter. Turn into two well-greased round cake pans and bake about 20 minutes, until the top is golden. Serve hot from the oven, top with butter.

Crackers

4 cups flour
1 1/2 teaspoons cream of tartar
1 1/2 teaspoons baking soda
3 tablespoons melted butter
1 cup water
More flour if necessary

Preheat the oven to 375 degrees F. Combine the dry ingredients. Add the butter and water and mix into a very stiff dough. Roll 1/8 inch thick on a well-floured surface. Prick the surface with a fork and cut into squares or any shape you prefer. Place on a lightly greased baking sheet and bake about 10 minutes, until just beginning to brown.

Rye and Indian Bread

Editor's note:

On the frontier breads, cakes and puddings were often steamed instead of baked. This slow, moist cooking method produces tender corn breads and rich cake-like puddings. Read about microwave steaming in the section Cooking with these Recipes.

1 cup Indian Meal (corn meal)
1 1/3 cup boiling water
1/2 cup rye flour
1/8 teaspoon salt
1/3 cup molasses
2 tablespoons almost melted butter

Put the corn meal in a medium mixing bowl and pour the boiling water over it. Stir to blend and set aside to cool. Stir in the rest of the ingredients. Steam the bread on top of the stove or in the microwave.

Johnny Cakes

Editor's note:

There are many versions of how this recipe got its name. But the one that makes the most sense to me is that it is a variation of "journey cake," as it is made from the ingredients most travelers would have on the wagons coming west. This is easily cooked over a campfire with extra made for pioneers to eat during the day until they stopped for the night and were able to cook their evening meal.

1 cup corn meal
1 cup milk
1/4 cup flour
1 1/2 teaspoons molasses
1/2 teaspoon baking soda

Preheat oven to 425 degrees F. Heat the milk until just below boiling. Stir in the corn meal and set aside until cool. Stir in the rest of the ingredients. Mix well. Pour into a lightly greased baking pan; an 8-inch square pan or pie pan will work well. Bake until browned and firm in the center, about 25 minutes.

OCTOBER 10, 1860

Rice Cakes

While in the West Indies, I was treated once or twice a day to rice cakes in the form of griddlecakes and became exceedingly fond of them. They are easily made and very easy, also, of digestion, and would not harm even a sick person.

—*From a Prairie Farmer reader*

1 1/2 cups cold cooked rice
(not "converted" or instant rice varieties)
1/2 cup milk
1/4 cup flour
1 egg

Combine all ingredients. Heat your frying pan or griddle as for pancakes. Grease lightly with butter. Put a large spoon of batter on the pan and spread quickly so that it is only one grain of rice thick. Cook until lightly browned and the top surface appears dry. Turn and press down onto the pan to brown the other side. Cook until light brown. Serve hot. These are very good spread with jam or butter. They taste somewhat like French crepes, but are more substantial.

Graham or Brown Bread

Editor's note:

There is a later, more
refined, version of a quick
whole wheat loaf later
in this chapter. See the
January 10, 1886
Graham Bread recipe.

4 cups graham or whole wheat flour
1 cup corn meal
1 tablespoon salt (optional)
1 1/2 teaspoons baking soda
1/2 cup sorghum
1 cup buttermilk
1 egg
(There is no yeast in this bread.)

Preheat the oven to 350 degrees F. Combine
the graham flour, corn meal, salt and baking
soda in a large mixing bowl. Stir in the
sorghum, buttermilk and egg. Mix well and
pour into two well-greased loaf pans. Bake
45 minutes or until the bread is firm and a
tester in the center comes out clean. Cool in
pans for 10 minutes, then continue cooling
on a wire rack.

MAY 5, 1877

Muffins

THE PRAIRIE FARMER
DEVOTED TO
Agriculture, Horticulture, Mechanics, Educa-
tion, Home Interests, General News,
Markets, &c.

Published Weekly, in a neat octavo form of sixteen pages,
with an Index at the end of each volume (six months.)
Terms for the "Prairie Farmer" for 1863.
One Copy, one year..$2 00
Two Copies, one year...3 00
Ten Copies, one year, and one to Agent............................15 00
Subscriptions for six months at half rates.
☞ Appropriate Advertisements will be placed in the
FARMER for 15 cents per line of space, Nonpareil, each in-
sertion, in ADVANCE. Special Notices, leaded, preceding ad-
vertisement, twenty cents per line of space occupied.
A square comprises ten lines of space.
☞ The circulation of the PRAIRIE FARMER is now the
largest of any paper of its class in the West and North-West,
and offers to Nurserymen, Florist, and implement Manufac-
turers, the best medium to reach the masses interested.
EMERY & CO., 204 Lake st.,
Chicago, Ills.

2 eggs
1 1/2 cups milk
2 tablespoons very soft butter
3 cups flour
3 teaspoons baking powder
1/2 cup sugar
1/2 teaspoon salt

Preheat the oven to 375 degrees F. Combine
the eggs, milk and butter. Mix the flour,
baking powder, sugar and salt in a medium
bowl. Quickly stir in the liquid ingredients.
Beat well and bake in buttered muffin tins
until light brown, about 20 to 25 minutes.

English Buns

August 18, 1883
"What, is it you, my dear
Adrienne?"
"Ah Jane! How do you do?
How you have changed!"
"I am married."
"Indeed! Are you happy?"
"Oh, but ... and you?"
"I am a widow."
"I have noticed that you
always have more luck
than I do."

1 package instant dry yeast
1/2 cup warm water
1 tablespoon sugar
1 cup butter, softened
1 cup brown sugar
3 eggs
6 to 8 cups bread flour

Proof the yeast by combining it with the warm water and tablespoon of sugar. Set aside until it is bubbly. Mix together the butter, brown sugar and eggs. Stir in the yeast and begin adding the flour. Continue until you have a smooth dough. Add the last cup by kneading it in. (You may mix this dough in a food processor.) Put dough in a clean bowl and set aside to rise until doubled. Punch down and form into buns about 2 inches in diameter. Place them on a lightly greased cookie sheet. Allow to rise until double. While the bread is rising, preheat the oven to 350 degrees F. Bake about 20 minutes, until browned and the rolls sound hollow when tapped.

Oatmeal Muffins

1 1/2 cups uncooked oatmeal
1/2 cup corn meal
1 cup flour
2 tablespoons sugar
1 teaspoon baking soda
1 2/3 cup sour milk

Preheat oven to 400 degrees F. Combine dry ingredients. Quickly stir in the milk and mix until just blended. Spoon batter into well-greased muffin tins. Bake until light brown, about 15 minutes.

Biscuits

2 cups buttermilk
1/4 cup cream
2 teaspoons baking soda
6 cups flour

January 6, 1859
A sermon in four words:
Shrouds have no pockets.

Preheat the oven to 425 degrees F. Combine the liquid ingredients. Put the flour in a large bowl, add the liquid mixture and begin mixing with your hands until you have a stiff, nonsticky dough. Knead for 5 minutes. (You may make this in your food processor with the plastic dough blade.) Pat out 1 inch thick, cut in rounds and place on lightly greased baking sheet. Bake 10 to 15 minutes until browned.

AUGUST 8, 1885

Steamed Rolls

Make a biscuit dough leaving out the shortening. Roll out 1/2-inch thick. Put a layer of any kind of fruit or berries and roll up. Set it in a steamer or put a can in a kettle to hold up the plate. Steam three-quarters of an hour.
—From a new reader.

SEPTEMBER 14, 1885

Spoon Corn Bread

We make a good kind of corn bread that remains moist two or three days. Take 2 teacupfuls of Indian meal, 3 1/4 cups of flour, 1 quart thick sour milk, 1 teacupful of molasses, a teaspoon each of soda and salt. Add the soda to the milk and molasses, stir in the flour and meal, and put into a deep basin that will admit of its rising one-third or more. Steam an hour and a half and bake an hour. If not convenient to steam, bake only an hour or two.
—Mrs. Collins

Spoon Corn Bread

A Southern housekeeper who has for years studied the art of providing inexpensive, and at the same time palatable, meals for a family would like to enter the Improvement Club.

Here is her recipe for Breakfast Corn Bread: Beat up two eggs, one pint each of sour milk and meal, a little salt and a level teaspoonful of soda; mix thoroughly; then stir in a small tablespoon of melted lard and another pint of milk. Pour into a tin pan and bake in a moderately hot oven until done through.

We call it spoon bread, as we send it to the table in the pan and use a spoon in serving it. My family prefers it to biscuits. There are several ways of making corn bread, all economical and good enough to eat.

Pumpkin or Apple Bread

Editor's note:

This recipe speaks volumes about 1880s life in a prairie kitchen. First, pumpkins continued to be an important and readily available ingredient. Apples are treated as the more rare of the two. Even though it was possible to purchase commercial yeast, the homemade variety is specified. Most every homemaker would have her own starter at hand. This is a heavy bread, note the long rising time. And, finally, the stove was "on" all night with a banked-down fire, to keep the bread warm overnight.

For a change, we are fond of pumpkin bread. Stew and strain the pumpkin and work in with it corn meal and sometimes a third wheat flour. To a quart of the strained pumpkin add a teaspoon salt, half a cup sugar, and a teacupful of homemade yeast. Some may prefer less sugar. Mix stiff as can be stirred with a spoon. Put it in a deep pan like those used for Boston brown bread. Let it rise for two or three hours and then bake in a slow oven. It is well to leave it in the oven over night to be ready warm for breakfast. Apples can be substituted for the pumpkin.
—Mrs. Finley

Sally Lunn

1 package instant dry yeast
1 teaspoon sugar
1/2 cup warm water
3 eggs
2 cups milk
2 tablespoons butter, melted
6 cups all-purpose flour

Combine the yeast, sugar and water and set aside until the mixture bubbles. Combine the eggs, milk and melted butter in a large mixing bowl. Stir in the yeast mixture and begin adding the flour, cup by cup. The dough will be softer than bread dough. Set aside to rise until double. Stir down and put into a lightly greased tube or bundt pan. Allow to rise until double. Preheat oven to 350 degrees F. Bake the Lunn until browned and the loaf sounds hollow when tapped, about 45 minutes. Remove from pan and allow to cool on a rack. Note that the original recipe calls for the stiffly beaten egg whites to be folded into the batter. Clearly the egg whites would not hold their fluff during the two risings. I have made the Lunn with the eggs going in whole.

Puffets

2 cups flour
1 tablespoon sugar
1 1/2 teaspoons baking powder
1 cup milk
1 egg
2 tablespoons very soft butter

Preheat the oven to 375 degrees F. Combine the flour, sugar and baking powder in a medium-sized mixing bowl. Combine the milk, egg and butter in a large measuring cup. Blend the two mixtures together and stir until just blended. Lightly grease gem muffin cups. Bake until lightly browned, about 20 minutes. Makes 2 dozen.

Graham Bread

2 cups light cream (half and half)
2 teaspoons vinegar
1/2 cup brown sugar
2 cups graham (whole wheat) flour
1 cup regular flour (not bread flour)
1 teaspoon baking soda

Editor's note:

This bread tastes very much like a yeast whole wheat loaf, but is made in a fraction of the time. We are used to having quick breads be sweet; this is heartier. The light nutty flavor of this bread makes it perfect for toasting, or serving with a cheese spread.

Preheat the oven to 350 degrees F. Make sour cream by combining the cream and vinegar in a medium-sized mixing bowl. Let it stand about 5 minutes until curdled. Add the brown sugar, flours and baking soda. Mix well with a spoon. Pour batter into lightly greased bread pans. Bake until the loaves are lightly browned, pulling away from the side of the pan and firm in the center, about 45 to 55 minutes. Cool in pans about 5 minutes before removing to cool on a wire rack.

Graham Cream Cakes

1 cup light cream
1/2 cup sugar
1 egg
1 3/4 cup graham flour
1 teaspoon baking powder
1/4 cup currants

Preheat the oven to 375 degrees F. Mix the cream and sugar, add the egg. Blend in the flour and baking powder and finally stir in the currants. Pour batter into lightly greased gem or mini-muffin pans. Bake about 15 to 20 minutes, until light brown, and the cream cakes have begun to pull away from the sides. Makes two dozen cakes.

Nice Rolls

1/3 cup butter
2 cups milk
1 package dry yeast
1/4 cup warm water
1 tablespoon sugar
8 cups flour
1/4 cup brown sugar
2 eggs

Bring the milk just to a boil and add the butter. Set aside to cool. Proof the yeast by adding it to the water and the tablespoon of sugar. Make a soft sponge by mixing 2 cups flour with the yeast and milk mixtures. Cover the bowl and set in a warm place until it begins to rise, about 15 minutes. Stir it down and add the eggs and remaining flour to make a dough that is not sticky. Knead until it is smooth and elastic. Put the dough in a clean, lightly greased bowl, cover it and set it aside in a warm place to rise until double. Punch the dough down. Form rolls by pinching off about 1/4 cup of dough for each roll and forming it into an oblong shape. Place on a lightly greased cookie sheet and let rise until double. Preheat oven to 350 degrees F. Bake until light brown, about 20 minutes.

Muffins

2 cups flour
1 1/2 teaspoons baking powder
2 teaspoons sugar
1/8 teaspoon salt
1 cup milk
2 eggs, separated

Preheat the oven to 375 degrees F. Combine the flour, baking powder, sugar and salt in a medium mixing bowl. Stir the egg yolks and milk together and add to the dry ingredients and mix until just combined. Beat the egg whites until they are stiff in a grease-free bowl. Fold into the batter. Lightly grease gem muffin pans and divide the batter among them. Bake until lightly browned, about 20 minutes. Makes 2 dozen.

Parker House Rolls

2 cups milk
1 package instant yeast
1/2 cup warm water
2 teaspoons sugar
2 cups bread flour
1 egg
1/2 cup very soft, almost melted, butter
4 cups additional bread flour
2 tablespoons more melted butter
1 egg yolk
2 tablespoons milk

Editor's note:

In the late summer and early fall of 1886, there was a lively correspondence in the pages of *Prairie Farmer* among readers seeking the recipe for rolls served at a Boston hotel. The difinitive Parker House rolls recipe was sent in by Clara Francis, *Prairie Farmer* food columnist in the 1870s. As the editor in 1886 wrote, "Clara Francis sends this recipe for making rolls, which she considers very fine. She obtained it in the *Prairie Farmer* six years ago."

Scald the milk and set aside to cool. Combine the yeast with the warm water and sugar. When it starts to bubble, mix it with the milk and first 2 cups flour. Set this sponge aside until it starts to bubble. Then stir it down, add the egg, butter and remaining flour until you have a dough that will not stick to the sides of the bowl. Knead it until smooth and elastic. Put it in a lightly greased bowl and grease the top of the dough. Cover and set aside until it is double. Punch it down and form the rolls.

Lightly flour a surface and put the dough on it. Roll out to 1 inch thick. Cut circles about 2 inches in diameter. Flatten the center of each circle with the rolling pin until it is quite thin. Brush half of each dough circle with melted butter. Fold it over, not quite meeting at the edges. Make a deep indentation on the rounded side of the roll with your fingers or the edge of the rolling pin. Place on a lightly greased baking sheet to rise until double. Preheat the oven to 350 degrees F. When the rolls are double in size, brush them with the egg yolk and milk mixture. Bake until golden brown on top and firm, about 25 minutes.

Domestic Economy

A male reader writes:

Domestic economy or household economy hardly receives its full share of attention in the Prairie Farmer. Much hard labor performed by the women could be avoided I think. Thus far in my journey through life, I find a vast difference in housekeepers. Some of them give us hot bread, hot coffee, fried meat, in fact everything hot three times a day; and others make it a rule to have light bread on hand and give us something hot occasionally. And you look into the kitchen of those who do the most cooking and they have the fewest utensils and conveniences to work with.

I sat at one table for about five months without seeing any light or even cold bread or meat of any kind, and the amount of kitchen furniture was about two or three skillets and a pot. They had a large farm and (were) well-to-do in the world with an interesting family around them, but they did not take the papers.

Editor's note:

You will find the recipe for Farmers Rice Pudding in the Cookies and Desserts section.

Now I would ask if so much hot food is healthy and is so much cooking necessary? And I would ask all our agricultural societies if not a good loaf of light bread is not as well worth a premium as a piece of jeans, a pair of socks, a pretty quilt, butter or cheese? And a well-kept farm house as much of a premium as a well-kept farm. Can they offer them no inducements to study domestic economy and make improvements in house keeping. Or are they perfect now and provided with everything for their comfort and convenience that is necessary for them to do their work with ease, or are such things less trifling to demand our attention? The ladies can speak for themselves, for there must be some in our state that are able to do so.

Give me the Sucker girl who can set the best table, with the least labor and expense, especially on a Sunday, which ought to be a day of rest, But is it? And now, if my aunties will not laugh at me, I will give you a recipe for Sunday supper that is good enough for me. Light bread, roast meat of any kind or boiled ham, pickles, baked or stewed fruit of any kind — all cold (cooked on Saturday) with buttermilk, sweet milk and water, if on hand. And for weather cold enough for fire, I would add hot boiled or baked potatoes. For dessert, pie of any kind, except flesh and Farmers Rice Pudding.

The man that would not put up with that should take a trip to California by the overland route.

Indian Corn for the Household

From the Housekeeper's Improvement Club:

We believe we are not amiss when we say that in the ordinary family not more than one pound of corn meal is used to 10 of wheat flour, though corn meal costs less than half as much. A pound or bushel of corn is about as good as wheat for working and fattening animals and our bodies are similar to those of our animals.

If we ate more corn, we would thus reduce the cost of living a good deal. But the trouble with a good many is that they do not know how to cook it so as to make it as acceptable as wheat. To do our share towards obviating this latter difficulty, we devote the whole space of this department the present week to the subject of dishes prepared from corn and trust that it will be of use to thousands of our members.

Tea Rusks

Rusks made without yeast are so much more quickly made than with it, that I generally prefer them for warm weather.

—Mrs. Ferris

3/4 cup sugar
2 tablespoons butter
2 eggs
1 cup milk
3 cups flour
3 teaspoons baking powder

Preheat the oven to 350 degrees F. Combine the butter and sugar. Stir in the eggs and mix well. Add the baking powder and half the flour. Stir in the milk and then the remaining flour. Drop by large spoonfuls onto lightly greased baking sheets. Bake about 20 minutes, until lightly brown and firm. Serve hot.

Hoe Cake and Why So Named

This good corn meal cake is always associated in my mind with a new country and an open fire with a scant supply of baking pans. In this emergency, the useful hoe came into requisition to lay the cake on and bake before the bright coals on the hearth. I believe this is the origin of the name.

Scald a quart of Indian meal in sufficient water to make a pretty thick batter. Add to it 2 tablespoons butter or shortening, a teaspoon of soda and 2 of salt. Beat well. Bake 30 to 40 minutes in a greased pan.

—Mrs. Wilson

Bread Making

From the Housekeeper's Improvement Club:

I never miss an article on bread making. With us it is the staff of life, and with good bread I am never worried if we are out of cake or pie. The wife and mother who has no one to help her must systemize the regular routine of the housework so that it may be off her hands and mind as much of the time as possible.

I began very young to take charge of the work of a farm house and dairy. I was often at my wit's end to get through the first part of the week the men ate so much bread. I used soft yeast, but always sponged my bread at night and kneaded it down in the morning. A young cousin from California visited us and at the first meal she said, "Oh, you make as good bread as my mother does," and her mother was a noted cook. I wondered if her mother was as glad as I was when the bread was out of the oven and done.

Three years later, the mother visited us and, after our greetings were over, I inquired into that bread matter and found her method was so simple. At supper time she boiled 6 very large potatoes in 2 quarts of water, mashed the potatoes through a colander, and added the water in which they were boiled and 1 pint of soft yeast. She turned this into the pan of flour and kept it warm. When her work was done up, she added sufficient wetting to this mixture, kneaded it thoroughly and left it until morning. Her bread pans were greased overnight and in the morning she arose early and lightly molded out the bread. When the oven was hot, the bread was usually ready and the day begun with your baking out of the way. I tried this way and was greatly delighted with the result.

—Dora Dean

Potato Bread

2 good-sized red potatoes
(about 1 pound)
1 quart water
2 packages instant dry yeast
1/2 cup warm water
1 tablespoon sugar
9 to 10 cups bread flour

Peel the potatoes and cut into chunks. Cook them in the quart of water until tender. Drain the water and save. Mash the potatoes and combine with the saved water. (I find a potato ricer works very well for this step.) Set aside to cool until lukewarm. Proof the yeast by combining it with the warm water and sugar and setting it aside. When the yeast is bubbly, combine it with the potatoes and begin adding the flour. After 6 or 7 cups, the dough will be stiff enough to begin kneading in the rest of the flour. Continue kneading until the dough is smooth and elastic. Put it in a lightly greased bowl and set aside in a warm place to rise until double. Punch the dough down and divide into four pieces. Form each into a loaf and put into lightly greased pans or make into free-form circular loaves and place on baking sheets. Let rise until double again. Preheat the oven to 350 degrees F and bake 35 to 40 minutes, until loaves are light brown and sound hollow when tapped.

How to Make Potato Yeast

From the Housekeeper's Improvement Club:

I have long read your valuable paper and am much interested in the recipes given in the Housekeeper's Improvement Club. I have tasted many of them and find them very valuable indeed. Herewith are the directions for making potato yeast which I have found to be very good: Take 4 raw potatoes, pare and grate fine; pour about 8 quarts of hot water on them and stir over a slow fire until boiling. Steep a handful of hops in a pint of water on the stove a few minutes; strain and add the hop water to the potatoes and stir. When so cool that it will not scald the yeast, add 1 cake or 1 cup of yeast, 1/2 a cup of salt and 1 cup brown sugar. Let it rise in a warm place for 6 to 8 hours. When it has thoroughly fermented put in cans or jars and set way in a cool place. Made in this manner, I have had it keep perfectly good for six weeks during the warmest season. One pint of this yeast will make 6 ordinary loaves of bread.

CHAPTER TWO

Eggs & Cheese

Today most of us think of eggs, milk, butter and cheese as ingredients, but in the early pages of *Prairie Farmer* they were most often presented simply as products from the farm. There were more lines written on how to preserve eggs through the winter and transport fancy molded butter to town than there are recipes featuring them. You'll find some of those articles in this chapter and others.

Certainly farm wives served up breakfasts with scrambled, boiled or fried eggs, but there were very few specific egg recipes in the magazine. There were, however, many articles on cooking without eggs: Cake without Eggs, Cookies without Eggs. Con-

> *"Raising eggs will pay — pay infinitely better than raising wheat or even corn if you engage in it systematically."*
> **Prairie Farmer, January 1853**

versely, underscoring the variability of the supply, there were many recipes that used up lots of eggs. Angel food and golden cakes each required a dozen, and custards used up vast quantities of milk or cream and eggs.

Omelet recipes began to appear in the late 1860s. Try several of the unusual ones we've included in this chapter. The 1877 recipe for hard-boiled eggs solves the problem of how to keep the filling nice for a picnic before the invention of aluminum foil and resealable plastic containers, and once again demonstrates the value of the early *Prairie Farmer* homemaking columns.

From the Du Page Co. Observer:

We should think some of the enterprising farmers of DuPage County, especially those residing near the railroad, would enter largely into the business of raising hens, for the purpose of supplying the Chicago market with eggs. These tender but indispensable things now readily bring 16 to 18 cents per dozen in that market and we have no doubt they are scarce at that price. Gentlemen, it will pay — pay infinitely better than raising wheat, or even corn, if you engage in it systematically.

SEPTEMBER, 1853

Preserving Eggs

"Have we a sure mode of keeping eggs?" There have been innumerable recipes published first and last, all of which fail somewhere, tho some of them answer a purpose.

The editor of the Maine Farmer says he has discovered one thing, and that is the "eggs to keep fresh must be fresh when packed," a truth which we spoke out to him years ago; but then the old question still remains.

The Agricultural Gazette has a mode, which for the family is about all that is needed, if it proves good, though for uses of sale it would amount to nothing.

It is thus: "Take a 1/2-inch board of any convenient length and breadth and pierce it as full of holes (each 1 1/2 inches in diameter) as you can, without risking the breaking of one hole into another. I found that a board of 2 feet 6 inches in length and 1 foot broad has 5 dozen in it — say 12 rows of five each.

Then take four strips of the same board of 2 inches broad and nail them together edgewise into a rectangular frame the same size as your board. Nail the board upon the frame, and the work is done, unless you choose, for the sake of appearances, to nail a beading of 3/4 inch round the board on the top. This looks better and sometime may prevent an egg from rolling off.

Put your eggs in this board as they come in from the poultry-house, the small end down, and they will keep good for six months if you take the following precautions. Take care that the eggs do not get wet either in the nest or afterwards. (In summer, hens are fond of laying among the nettles or long grass and any eggs taken from such nests in wet weather should be put away for immediate use.) Keep them in a cool room in summer and out of the reach of frost in the winter, and then I think the party trying the experiment will have abundant reason to be satisfied with it.

Tomato Omelet

Editor's note:

This recipe began with an editor's comment that it was "nice with beefsteak."

1 quart chopped peeled tomatoes
2 onions, chopped
(Or use one 16-ounce can
stewed tomatoes.)
1/2 teaspoon cayenne pepper
1/3 cup fresh bread crumbs
5 eggs stiffly beaten
2 tablespoons butter

Make a fresh tomato sauce by combining the tomatoes and onions in a large saucepan. Simmer 1 hour, stirring occasionally. To save time and some effort, use a can of stewed tomatoes, heated. Add cayenne pepper and the fresh bread crumbs to the tomatoes. Melt 2 tablespoons butter in a large frying pan. Put the tomato mixture into the pan. Add the eggs; continue cooking over low to medium heat until the eggs are set. Fold the omelet in half and serve.

DECEMBER 13, 1860

Composition for Preserving Eggs

Here is a receipe which a friend gave us the other day: Take half a bushel of quick lime and put in a tub, and slack it with hot water till it becomes of the thickness of cream; then add 3 1/2 pounds salt and 1/2 pound cream of tartar. Stir them together; then store your eggs in kegs or barrels and pour in the preparation when cold till the eggs are entirely covered. This quantity is enough to keep one barrel of eggs. If the cask is kept tight, the eggs, it is asserted, will keep 18 months or two years.

How to Prepare Bonemeal

This is how to do it says a correspondent of the New Hampshire Journal of Agriculture:

With a sledge hammer, break the bones into pieces of 1, 2 or 3 inches. Take a hogshead tub, put in 2 or 3 inches of hard wood ashes, the same depth of bones, then ashes, then bones until full. Pound or press solid as convenient, fill with water or urine, all that it will absorb. If done in the spring or summer, by the next spring it will shovel out fully decomposed, the bones being as soft as chalk.

Then if you have it, add all your hen manure, shovel and rake it over once a week, for three of four weeks before planting time; by that time it will be finely powdered. Put about equal to a handful of the compost into a hill of corn, potatoes, squashes, melons, &c. when it will be found to forward the crops to a wonderful degree.

Jam Omelet

4 egg whites
6 egg yolks
1 tablespoon butter
2 to 4 tablespoons tart jam
(such as plum or red currant)
Confectioner's sugar

August 18, 1883
"Well, may I hope then, dearest, that at some time I may have the happiness of making you my wife."
"Yes, I hope so, I am sure," she said. "I am getting tired of suing fellows for breach of promise."

Beat the egg whites and yolks until very frothy. Melt the butter in a frying pan or omelet pan and when it is bubbly add the eggs. Cook until the eggs are set. Gently spread the jam on the top of the eggs, and fold the omelet in half. Slide it out onto a heat-proof dish. Dust the top with confectioner's sugar and put it under the broiler to brown.

Puff Omelet

3 tablespoons melted butter
3 tablespoons flour
1 cup milk
1/2 teaspoon pepper
6 eggs, separated

Preheat the oven to 350 degrees F. Make a white sauce by melting the butter in a small saucepan. Add the flour and cook until bubbly. Gradually stir in the milk; cook until the white sauce is thickened. Add the pepper. Beat the yolks and whites separately. Add a little of the hot white sauce to the egg yolks to bring them up to heat, then add them to the rest of the white sauce. Fold the sauce into the stiffly beaten egg whites. Pour the omelet mixture into a soufflé dish that is lightly greased and coated with bread crumbs. Bake 35 to 45 minutes. Serve immediately.

Nun's Toast

6 hard-boiled eggs
(peeled and sliced into rounds)
1 tablespoon butter
1 tablespoon minced onion
1 tablespoon flour
1 cup milk
Salt and pepper to taste
Four slices of toasted bread

For two servings: Cut the eggs into rounds and set aside. In a medium saucepan, melt the butter and add the onion. Cook until the onion is transparent, but not browned. Add the flour and cook until bubbly. Add the milk and cook, stirring until the sauce is thickened. Add salt and pepper. Add the eggs, and mix very gently. Divide the mixture over the toast in two dishes and serve.

Baked Omelet

6 eggs
1 tablespoon butter
Salt and pepper to taste

To make a Sweet Omelet, substitue
4 tablespoons sugar and
1 teaspoon vanilla
for the salt and pepper.

Preheat the oven to 350 degrees F. Put a baking dish in the oven to preheat. Beat the egg whites until stiff. Lightly beat the egg yolks with the pepper and salt. Fold the egg yolks into the whites. Pour the egg mixture into the preheated dish and put it into the oven. Bake 20 minutes or until the eggs are set and puffed. Serve immediately.

Welsh Rarebit

1/2 pound rich cheese
(Cheddar, Swiss or Colby)
2 eggs, well beaten
1 teaspoon sharp mustard
1 tablespoon butter
1/2 cup cream

Grate the cheese and mix with other ingredients in the top of a double boiler. Cook, stirring, until the cheese is melted and the whole becomes smooth and soft. To serve, spread over slices of nicely browned toast and serve hot.

To Keep Butter

Mr. N.H. Foster, McHenry County, informs us that he keeps butter for market as follows.

He provides tight barrels as for pork or lard. After salting and working the butter till it is in first-rate order, it is made into rolls and packed in the barrels. As fast as put down, a good brine is poured over it till the rolls are covered with it, a weight being kept upon them to prevent them from rising. When the barrel is full, it is headed up and kept till fresh butter is a scarce article in market, when it is as good as the day it was put down and will sell for a prime article for table use.

It deserves to be said that butter so kept will lose about 10 pounds in 100, but will commonly bring price enough to make it up, especially to such as are distant from market.

Ham Omelet

2 tablespoons butter
1/2 cup ham, chopped fine
6 eggs, well beaten
2 tablespoons fresh parsley, minced

Melt the butter in a large frying pan over medium heat. Add the ham and sauté until heated through without browning, being careful not to burn the butter. Add the eggs. Cook over medium heat, stirring frequently until the eggs are just set. Toss in the parsley and serve.

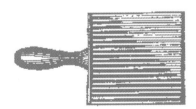

Deviled Eggs

 *Editor's note:*

The prairie farmers served deviled eggs at picnics and luncheons just as we serve them today. However, the way the eggs were "deviled" is somewhat different. Beginning with the basic hard-boiled egg, these folks did as we do, use handy ingredients to make the eggs special. Where it is a simple matter for us to open the ever-present jars of mayonnaise or salad dressing and mustard, the earliest cooks needed to make not only the mayonnaise, but the mustard as well. So recipes for deviled eggs through the 1870s have the mashed egg yolks combined with equal amounts of minced ham or other meats and even vegetables, whatever was handy and easy.

These practical folks also wrote of ways to solve the transportation problem of the softly filled eggs.

AUGUST 18, 1877

Hard Boiled Eggs

Hard boiled eggs will help to make a nice variety for the picnic. Boil them for ten minutes, then plunge into cold water. Just before they are put in the baskets, remove the shells; wipe the eggs dry and cut each one in two lengthwise. Sprinkle plentifully with salt and pepper, then join and wrap each egg in fringed tissue paper.

—Clara Francis

JUNE 9, 1888

Deviled Eggs

Another nice luncheon dish is made of eggs as follows. Boil half a dozen eggs or more until hard, put them in cold water so that they can be shelled easily. Then from the side, scoop out a piece of white and the whole of the yolk. Rub the latter smooth, season with salt and pepper, prepared mustard, oil or melted butter and a little vinegar. When well mixed, push this mixture back into the yolk cavities. Garnish the dish with parsley and pieces of the white.

—Mrs. Howe

Poultry Notes

Nearly every year for the past ten years I have told the Prairie Farmer readers how to preserve eggs, and have often asked those who called for the information to report their success, but it is seldom that I hear from one of them. Now I wish everybody who packed eggs last summer for win-ter use would take time to tell us of their success or failure. You needn't make along story of it; just tell us when you packed them, how, where they were kept, when used and in what condition they were. You can get it all on a postal card.

—Fanny Field, poultry notes editor

Eighty by One Hundred and Sixty

To the editors of Prairie Farmer:

Please find below a detailed account of a crop raised on prairie sod. The size of the lot is 80 feet by 160 feet — a little less than 50 square rods. It was plowed and planted for the first time in the year 1867. The corn averaged 13 feet, 6 inches in height:

72 bushes of corn	$16.50
13 bushels of Tilden tomatoes	22.60
Sold tomato plants	6.00
3 bushels potatoes	6.25
Green cucumbers	3.00
2 barrels of pickles	21.00
1 bushel peppers	3.00
1 bushel citrons	1.25
1 bushel white beans	3.00
Sold corn fodder	1.00
Lettuce sold	2.00
Cabbage plants	2.00
Total	$87.60

The above crop was raised in Monee in Will County, Ill.,
by the subscriber L. Easterbrooks.

Cistern

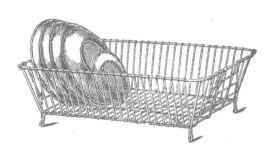

Soft water in the kitchen is a good thing, especially a constant supply for summer and winter. The rich can have it for they build large cisterns as part of the house — not so in the country. On the approach of a summer shower, the whole household must be astir, for the water for the next washing must be saved; wash tubs, old barrels and pails must be set out to catch the water dripping from the eaves; hastily improvised boards must be put up to assist in the work. A drought of two or three weeks starts the wooden hoops and the water runs through the staves like a sieve, a gust of wind and down come the boards.

Every farmer's wife and daughter will agree with us that no kitchen is complete without a good cistern, and that cistern is not complete without it has a good anti-freezing pump. With such a pump in good order, the water is alike available in summer and winter.

Mrs. Jones, as the readers of the Farmer all know, is a progressive woman and wide awake to all labor-saving contrivances, has a plan that she had just been illustrating. Going into the kitchen she says, "Suppose you get a large cask — an old wine or ale pipe — that will hold 2 or 3 barrels of water; set this in the corner opposite the cistern. Get an anti-freezing force pump; attach this to a lead pipe that shall run under the porch and up through the walls of the house, and in at the top of the cask. Put a large faucet in the barrel so that the discharge will be rapid. A few minutes' work of the husband or the boys at the pump will suffice to fill the cask, when the wife or daughter can draw at eight for the washing. A small bench, wash basin and towel would set off the cask to good advantage, and often to more cleanliness among the junior members of the family."

We need not repeat that the usual difficulty in obtaining assistance in the house demands all the aid that genius can invent or that mechanism, can supply.

If the spinning wheel and the old hand loom, the demand for linen shirts, two cloth pants and frocks were restored to the household, there would a lively rebellion among its inmates. And if the old water trough, that was so prolific in wrigglers and mosquitoes with the outdoor oven and leach-tub were added, we dare not predict the result.

Transporting Butter

From the Grocery and Provision Review:

A good way to carry rolls of butter over a rough road or any other is to make tin boxes to suit the size of the rolls, cylindrical in form like a pill box, but dividing near the middle so that the cover will constitute one-half of the box.

Wrap each roll in fine bleached muslin and insert one end in the box and slide to cover over the other end, pressing it down until the end of the roll will touch the inside of the cover. Enclose the tin boxes in a wooden one. Make the wooden box of sound 1 1/2-inch boards, fastening the corners firmly with sheet-iron straps. The outside should be planed and painted; the inside may be rough.

Line the inside of this box with two thicknesses of felt with thin but sound boards, nailing them right through the felt snugly to the outside boards.

The felt is a nonconductor and will keep the heat from striking though into the butter. Line the inside of the cover to the wooden box in the same way, cleating the top of it to prevent warping or splitting, and attach it to the box by strong hinges on one side and hold the other down firmly by two straps and staples. Stout handles should be put upon each end of the box for convenience in handing. Rolls of butter in tin boxes enclosed in such a case will neither get out of shape nor feel the heat.

Upon arrival at the end of their journey the rolls are easily removed from the tin boxes, which can be returned to their case. Boxes 4 1/4 inches in diameter and 8 inches long hold a roll of 4 pounds and cost from $1.50 to $2 per dozen, according to the quality of tin. The whole outfit is cheap, durable and convenient, and will secure an attractive form to the butter upon its reaching the market.

CHAPTER THREE

Soups

Prairie homemakers were under just as many economic and time pressures as we are today. It is not surprising that soup recipes run the range from a two-day process involving making stock from scratch, taking advantage of all kitchen scraps, to soups made quickly from previously canned or purchased ingredients.

Several recipes in this collection also provide timesavings by making two dishes at once, an entrée and a soup, either for use as a first course or to be set aside for supper later in the week. The recipe Green Corn Soup (and a chicken dinner) from September 8, 1877, is a perfect example. It is one of the longest recipes in the book, but when finished, you have a fine chicken dinner, plus a pot of delicious soup.

My favorite recipe in this chapter is the May 12, 1877, Tomato Soup. It is delicious. It freezes well. It makes a very good sauce. I frequently simmer chicken parts in it and then reduce the sauce and add a bit of honey and more cayenne pepper to make a pan-barbecued dish. But what I like best about this recipe is that it really is so typical of the methods and flavors of the 19th century. The combination of bay, pepper, cinnamon, allspice and mace, so common for meats and soups on the prairie, has almost disappeared from our cooking palate.

Long simmering, straining and reducing concentrate the flavors. It is important to mash the tomato soup and other vegetable puree soups through a sieve by hand. Running it through a food processor will work, but there is a perceptual difference in the texture and even the flavor of the finished product. I enjoy the back and forth pressure of the wooden spoon against the sieve, or the rhythmic clink of the metal food mill. The time it takes gives opportunity to reflect on the generations of women who have prepared recipes like this and the value of good food, well prepared.

> *"If the good housewife would devote less time to the concoction of toothsome goodies and more to the making of nourishing broths, she would find not only an increase in bodily and mental activity, but a decrease in household expenses."*
> **Prairie Farmer, April 28, 1877**

Good Health

By A. Physician:

We believe profoundly in soup — in properly made soups we mean of course. Like many other products of the cuisine, if badly prepared, it is the bane of the dinner table, but rightly made it becomes, to a certain degree, a passport to health. Americans are not a soup-eating people, that is they do not make soup a standard article of diet. Many people of foreign countries exceed us in this, and in just about the same degree they exceed us in good health, good digestion and good serene tempers — not to say that it is wholly due to the soup they eat, much must with other habits of eating be attributed to this.

Pot Au Feu

Nothing so well symbolizes the economical habits of Continental Europe and especially France, as the pot au feu. This is an iron pot kept constantly simmering upon the fire, into which is put from day to day all the wholesome remnants of food, which in this country are thrown away. Our people in their magnificent way of doing things never stop to consider how much nutriment adheres even to well-picked bones of porterhouse steaks, mutton chops, ribs of beef, legs of mutton, etc.

All these and many things beside are put into the pot au feu. Water, seasoning and fragrant herbs are added as required and the constant simmering — a solvent for even the toughest of Texan beef — extracts every particle of marrow, and the bones come out as clean and white as if they had been bleached for years in the sun. Among the common people, more than half the nutriment for the day comes from the pot au feu, and if any member of the family comes home at an unusual hour hungry, it affords at all times a meal at once warm and wholesome.

This explains how, as Mrs. Hugh McCullock tells us, the 40 million of France could live on what the 40 million of America throw away. And when we consider the wretched cookery that prevails in this country, it is not too much to affirm that they could live quite as well as do our farmers and day laborers.

A Souperficial Talk

On an Important Detail in Household Economy:

Would that we could persuade housekeepers that the much-neglected soup possesses merits that should claim their attention. If, as a nation, we were less devoted to the inevitable "pie" we would not be, as we are, a nation of dyspeptics.

For every ten women who pride themselves on the puffiness of their puddings and cakes, the excellence of their sweetmeats and pies, there is not more than one that has other than the most primitive ideas in regard to soup. If the good housewife would devote less time to the concoction of toothsome goodies and more to the making of nourishing broths, and when the children come from school, give them a bowl of this to satisfy their hunger instead of allowing them to satiate their appetite with sweet things, she would find not only an increase in bodily and mental activity, but (also) a decrease in expenses.

In a family of average meat consumers, there are many odd bits which, with the addition now and then of a few pounds of the neck or foreshank of beef, or a knuckle of veal and an occasional vegetable pottage, would suffice to keep the table daily supplied with palatable and nutritious soup. And if judicious management is used, the manufacture of it need only consume a small portion of time.

—Clara Francis

Stock

The basis of stock should be lean uncooked meat: neck and foreshank of beef and veal of the best. To this add the scraps and bones, the latter cracked at every inch of their length. Allow 1 quart of cold water to every pound of meat. Put it on the fire without salt and heat slowly, and when it boils, skim thoroughly, add a little cold water and skim again.

Repeat until the liquid is perfectly clear, then add to every 5 quarts of water, 1 carrot, 1 small turnip, 2 onions stuck with 6 cloves, 2 heads celery, some bruised celery seed, 2 bay leaves, a dozen peppercorns and 6 stalks parsley. Cover and simmer slowly for five or six hours.

Strain through a fine sieve, put in jars and store in a cold place. If you wish a brown stock, fry some veal and vegetables with a piece of salt pork. When the stew pan is covered with a fine brown glaze, add the remaining meat and bones, cover with water and continue as before.

Tomato Soup

2 quarts fresh tomatoes, cut in quarters
(or a 6-ounce can of whole tomatoes)
2 onions, cut in half
1 carrot, sliced
I turnip, sliced
2 bay leaves
4 cloves, stuck in the onion
6 peppercorns
6 whole allspice berries
1 stick cinnamon
1/2 teaspoon mace
5 stalks celery
1 teaspoon sugar
Beef knuckle
Salt and pepper to taste
1 gallon water

Combine all the ingredients in a large soup kettle. Bring to a boil, reduce heat and simmer for 3 or 4 hours. Strain through a sieve. Wash out the kettle and return the soup to it. Let it simmer until it is the consistency of thick cream. Add cayenne pepper and vinegar to taste. Serve with croutons.

Nice Pork Soup

Put in soup tureen with pieces of stale (toasted) bread and you have a nice dish.

1 to 2 pounds pork steaks or chops
cut into 1-inch cubes
8 cups water
1 large onion, chopped
2 large potatoes, cut into cubes
(white or sweet)
2 carrots, thinly sliced
1 cup cream
3 tablespoons flour
1/2 teaspoon mace
1 teaspoon pepper
Salt to taste

Combine the pork, onion and water, bring to a boil, then lower the heat and simmer until the pork is very tender, skimming off the foam that comes to the top. When the meat is tender, add the potatoes and carrots and simmer until they are tender. Combine the cream and flour, add to the soup and stir until the soup is thickened.

Green Corn Soup (and a chicken dinner)

For the chicken dinner and the soup:
10 ears fresh corn
1 piece salt pork or 3 slices bacon, diced
1 chicken, cut into pieces
1 gallon cold water

For the chicken dinner:
1 cup milk
1 teaspoon pepper
1 teaspoon sage
1/2 teaspoon mace
2 tablespoons butter
2 tablespoons corn starch

For the soup:
1 cup cream
Salt and pepper to taste
2 tablespoons butter
2 tablespoons corn starch
2 tablespoons minced parsley

To begin: Cut the corn from the cob and set aside, reserving the cobs. Put the salt pork or bacon in a very large soup pot and cook slowly until browned. Put in the chicken and cook over medium heat until the pieces are browned. Carefully pour in 1 gallon (16 cups) of cold water and add the corn cobs without the kernels. Bring to a boil, lower the heat and simmer until the chicken is tender, about 45 minutes.

To finish the fricasseed chicken dinner: Take out the chicken, placing it on a large platter or casserole dish. Take out 2 cups of the cooking liquid and put it in a medium saucepan. Add 1 cup milk and the seasonings. Blend the butter with the cornstarch and stir in. When the sauce has thickened, pour it over the chicken.

To finish the soup: Strain the liquid remaining in the soup kettle, removing the corncobs. Return the liquid to the kettle, add the corn kernels and simmer gently until the corn is tender. (The original recipe suggests this would take an hour, I think with today's varieties of sweet corn, 5 to 10 minutes are more probable). Season with salt and pepper to taste. Combine the cornstarch and butter and stir into the soup with the cream and simmer until thickened slightly. The original suggests finishing the soup by "throwing in a little chopped parsley. A small knuckle of veal or the bones and scraps of fowls can be substituted for the whole fowl if more convenient."

Asparagus soup

1 pound asparagus
3 cups water
1 cup stock
1/2 tablespoon butter
1 tablespoon flour
1/2 cup cream
Salt and pepper to taste
1/2 tablespoon sugar

Chop the asparagus into 1-inch sections, keeping the tips separate. Boil the tips until tender in the water. Remove them and set them aside, then cook the rest of the stalks in the same water. Press the stalks through a strainer, or process in a food processor. Add the cooking water and stock. Combine the butter and flour and stir into the soup, simmering until it thickens slightly. Add the cream, salt and pepper and sugar. Heat until warm, but do not allow it to boil. Stir in the asparagus tips and serve.

MAY 12, 1877

Green Pea Soup without Meat

1 pound dried peas
2 quarts water

2 cups loosely packed shredded flavorful leaf lettuce such as bib
1 large cucumber, peeled, seeded and grated (about 1 cup)
1 1/2 cups finely diced onion
1 pint fresh green peas
1/4 pound fresh butter
Salt and pepper
Sprig of mint

For this soup you will be combining two vegetable mixtures, one made of fresh vegetables that have been sautéed, the other the dried peas that have been reconstituted.

Wash one bag of dried split peas and pick over. Combine with 2 quarts water and simmer until the peas are tender. In another pan, melt the butter and add the fresh vegetables. Sauté until the vegetables are tender. Push the fresh ingredients through a sieve and combine them with the dried pea mixture. Stir in finely shredded mint leaves just before serving.

Editor's note:

Although the period directions call for straining the fresh vegetables, you may add them whole for a chunkier soup rather than a puree.

Mulligatawny Soup

The best plan is to make this and all similar soups the day before they are needed and, when thoroughly cold, remove the fat, which will form a cake on the surface.

Beef or veal knuckle (soup bone)
1 pound beef chuck (or chicken or turkey)
3 carrots, peeled and sliced thinly
1 turnip, peeled and diced
3 medium onions, peeled and sliced thinly
3 tart apples, peeled, cored and chopped
6 peppercorns
6 whole allspice berries
1/4-pound slice of ham
(or 4 pieces of bacon, diced)
1 cup cold water
4 quarts more water
3 tablespoons curry powder
1 cup flour
1/2 teaspoon salt, optional
1 tablespoon sugar
1 lemon, thinly sliced
Boiled rice as an accompaniment

Put the soup bone, beef or other meat, carrots, turnip, onions, apples, peppercorns, allspice berries, ham and cup of cold water in a large, heavy stockpot. Cook over low heat, stirring frequently until the meat and vegetables are browned and the bottom of the pot has a browned glaze. Add the remaining water, bring to a boil, reduce heat and simmer until the meat is tender, about 3 hours. Strain the soup through a fine sieve; do not press. Set the ham and other meat aside and discard the rest of the vegetables and bones. Skim the fat off the soup. In a dry heavy frying pan or stockpot, combine the curry powder, flour, salt and sugar. Cook over medium heat until the flour just begins to brown. Gradually stir in the soup and let simmer until thick. Add the reserved beef, or other meat, cut into small squares. Serve, garnishing the bowls with slices of lemon. Guests add as much rice as they would like.

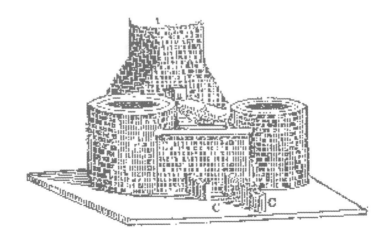

Iowa Housekeeper's Notes

Soup, when well made, is most nourishing and gives a pleasing variety to the table fare. In the plain homes of many farmers and working men, of course, little attention can be paid to a variety of courses in meal. The housewife, having generally all the cooking and the work of the household to attend to, cannot find time to make soup for dinner every day and prepare all the other dishes expected. Yet, occasionally, it is very nice for a change. But few other articles are really needed to make a hearty meal, when only enough relishable food is all that can be provided. Indeed, if more soup was used and less pie and cake, it would be better for health. I provide the following recipes.
—Mrs. Emma T. King, King's Ranch, Pottawattamie County, Iowa

Vegetable Soup

2 quarts beef or chicken stock
6 medium potatoes, peeled and chopped
2 turnips, peeled and chopped
1 onion, peeled and chopped
2 carrots, peeled and sliced
2 cups thinly sliced cabbage

Add the vegetables to the hot broth and simmer until they are tender.

Potato Soup

10 medium-sized potatoes
Salt pork or 5 slices of bacon, diced
2 onions, sliced
1 cup chopped celery
1 quart milk
1 tablespoon butter
Salt and white pepper to taste
1/4 cup fresh, chopped parsley,
for garnish

Peel and cut up the potatoes and boil them in water with the bacon, onions and celery until tender. Drain and press through a potato ricer, strainer or process in a food processor. Return to the soup pot. Add the milk, butter and seasonings. Bring just to a boil. It should be the consistency of thick cream. Put several small cubes of buttered toast or commercial croutons in the bottom of the bowl and pour the soup over.

Noodle Soup

For the noodles:
1 egg
1/4 teaspoon salt
1 cup or less flour

4 cups beef stock
Chopped parsley

Combine the egg and salt and add as much flour as it can take. Knead it well and roll out very thin. Coat lightly with flour, roll up and cut in thin slices. Drape them out flat and let them dry for about 1/2 hour. Drop them in boiling water and stir for about 2 minutes. Drain and put into simmering broth. Add a little chopped parsley and serve.

Julienne Soup

3 carrots
1 turnip
1 medium onion
3 stalks celery
1 tablespoon butter
4 cups beef stock

Peel the vegetables and cut into thin uniform matchsticks. Melt the butter in a medium saucepan and add the vegetables. Cook over low heat until the vegetables become limp and the onion turns golden. Add the beef stock and cook until the vegetables are tender. The amounts of vegetables can be adjusted to suit your preference.

Quick Bean Soup

2 regular-size cans white beans
2 cups light cream
2 tablespoons butter
1 teaspoon pepper

Drain the beans and rinse. Mash them through a sieve, or process in a food processor. Put them in a medium saucepan. Add the cream, butter and pepper. Cook, stirring frequently, until the soup is hot. You may garnish with chopped parsley.

Mock Oyster Soup

1 large can stewed tomatoes
6 cups milk
Salt and pepper to taste
2 cups crumbled crackers

Combine the tomatoes, milk and seasoning in a large saucepan. Bring just to a boil, stirring frequently. Pour over the crumbled crackers in a tureen or in individual bowls.

MARCH 21, 1886

Quick Soups of Tomato or Corn

This is a very convenient course when you have unexpected company. My children are so fond of it. I often serve it for their supper after they come home from school. —Mrs. Freeman

1 large can tomatoes, chopped or pureed
(or 2 regular-size cans corn)
2 cups water
2 cups hot milk
1/4 cup cracker crumbs or
Dry bread crumbs

Combine the canned vegetables with the water and simmer until they are very soft. Press them through a soup sieve or process in a food processor. Return to the soup pot, season with salt and pepper to taste, stir in the hot milk and the crumbs.

June 6, 1888
A Michigan girl had found
2,125 four-leaf clovers and
isn't married yet. An Omaha
girl who found out how to
make a pumpkin pie was
married in three months.

Clam Chowder

Clams in the West

I suppose the idea of giving directions for making clam chowder will seem odd to western housekeepers, but clams are now being supplied quite fresh and at reasonable prices in nearly all the larger cities and towns almost out to the Rocky Mountains. It seems so like our old Rhode Island ways that I often send for both oysters and clams in the shell when my husband goes to Chicago. They are little dearer than in the East.
—*Mrs. Kingston*

We get good canned oysters just as cheaply and just as good as we did 15 years ago when living only 23 miles from Fairview, Conn., the great oyster place. Husband says there are several restaurants in Chicago that supply only oysters, clams, lobsters, and other sea food with salt and fresh water fish. The direct railway facilities from Baltimore, Philadelphia and New York put these things down in Chicago quite fresh through refrigerator or ice cars. Will Mrs. Kingston tell how she prepares clam chowder? I know hers is good.
—*Mrs. Williams*

Mrs. Kingston's Clam Chowder

15 to 20 clams
(or 1 small can minced clams)
2 large potatoes, peeled and diced
1/2 onion, minced
2 cups water
1/8 teaspoon cayenne pepper,
or more to taste
3 tablespoons butter
3 tablespoons flour
6 cups hot milk
12 soda crackers, broken into pieces, but not crushed, or use 1 cup oyster crackers

If using fresh clams, scrub the shells until they are very clean and put the clams in a kettle. Pour over 2 cups water, cover and cook gently until the clams open. Remove the clams from their shells and chop fine. Combine them with the reserved cooking liquid and keep warm. Cook the potatoes and onion in the 2 cups water until very tender. Add the cayenne pepper, the cooked clams and enough of the cooking liquid to make it as salty as you prefer. If you are using canned clams, drain off the liquid and add some of it back into the mixture. Combine the butter and flour in a large saucepan. Cook over medium heat until the mixture bubbles. Gradually stir in the hot milk and cook until smooth and thickened, stirring frequently. Put the crackers in the bottom of a soup tureen. Pour in the clam and potato mixture and then very gradually the thickened hot milk. Stir and serve.

CHAPTER FOUR

Vegetables

Prairie Farmer advertising columns offered an abundance of seeds for the farm kitchen garden. "Collections of Vegetable Seeds by mail" with selections of 20 and 40 varieties appeared in early spring. Sweet potatoes, white potatoes, turnip seeds, rhubarb and strawberry plants were offered along with grape vines, peach and apple trees of all varieties. Spring of 1877 brought offers of Garrision's Early Favorite Tomato "without a doubt the earliest and best variety grown. Ripening July 12th to 20th."

Writers of the household columns wanted to make sure pioneering farm families ate their vegetables, too. Many of those columns during the first five decades of the magazine discussed the importance of vegetables to healthful eating. The vegetable recipes in *Prairie Farmer* were consistently simple in their approach. Unlike many of the cookbooks of the time that suggested cooking vegetables for very long times and serving them smothered in

> *"Whatever shall make vegetables more relishful will extend their popular use, and therefore any simple recipe for cooking them is a public good."*
> **Prairie Farmer, November 1846**

heavy sauces, here the cooking instructions were simple. *Prairie Farmer* writers stressed freshness and quick cooking to assure the best and most healthful preparation.

In the first five decades of *Prairie Farmer*, there are more recipes for tomatoes than any other vegetable, although cucumbers run a close second. Corn, tomatoes and pumpkins appear to be the vegetables prairie settlers most commonly grew and used in their kitchens. Corn could be served fresh, dried and ground or processed with lye to make hominy. Tomatoes could be "put-up" in a number of ways, and pumpkins, if not preserved, could be kept in the cold cellar. Potatoes, cabbages, cucumbers and beans were other favorite additions to the garden and storehouse. As the recipes in this chapter suggest, with these few vegetables prairie cooks had raw material to make a wide variety of dishes from appetizers and relishes to main dishes and even desserts throughout the year.

Breaking the Prairie

By D.A. Canton

Of course among the first objects was to get some prairie broken; and to that subject were my inquiries directed. What was the best season of the year in which to break prairie. How deep should it be broken. With what team could it be most profitably done, taking into account the expense and quality of the work. In answer to all of these questions, I received answers differing widely from each other, from men of perhaps equal experience and intelligence.

In reply to the first inquiry, some said commence breaking as soon as the ground is sufficiently dry in the spring, but be sure you stop the plowing by the first of July. Others assured me that no consideration should induce me to break except in the month of June; while others are continued into July as well as June and many assured me that breaking might profitably continue into September, should circumstances permit.

An equal contradictory opinion was observed in answer to the other inquiries. What was to be done amid such a variety of opinions — such a multitude of contradictory advice. Yet even here I found safety in a multitude of counsel. I pursued my inquiries and ascertained the reason assigned by each for the opinion which he gave and found that each consideration was deduced from a reasonable cause. But without going into the particular experience of each one, I will state briefly that the decisions I have arrived from my own experience and observations assisted by what I have been able to learn from others.

For a Spring Crop: If it be intended to raise a spring crop the first year and especially corn, it is advisable to start the plough as soon as the grass has started sufficient to afford a good bite. By this time in ordinary seasons the ground will be sufficiently dry and the plough may be kept going as late as it will do to put in the crop. The crop will be found to be best on land first broken, but the next year it will be found that the last broken will make the best condition.

For a Fall Crop: If a fall crop is intended, the breaking should not commence until about the first of June and may continue into the middle of August — in very dry seasons, perhaps a month later. It will almost invariable be found that the land first broken will have the best corn and nearly twice the quantity may be expected from land broken in June than will be realized from land broken in September. So that it will be readily perceived that if time can otherwise be profitably employed, it is not advisable to continue breaking so late at that time.

Crop on the sod: If it is proposed to raise a spring or fall crop on the sod, the prairie should by all means, be broken as deep as possible, say from four to five inches at least. All who have had experience in prairie farming are well aware that the ground is composed of a strong tenacious mass of grass roots so firmly interwoven together near the surface, of which there is comparatively but very little earthly substance to be found, and that little is so firmly compounded and bound up that it can afford but very little nourishment to the growing crop. Hence the necessity of plowing deep, in order to obtain sufficient mould to sustain the crop will be readily perceived. It is true that it requires a very considerable more force to break deep than it does to break shallow, perhaps more than would be at first imagined, but then you are compensated for that by the greater ease and facility with which the land is ploughed the second time. Because if the land is broken shallow, it is necessary to go below that first breaking when you cross-plough or split the furrows (which is perhaps the better practice), and hence you are compelled to cut off all of the old roots again while they are yet sufficiently strong to afford considerable resistance.

If no crop is intended to be grown the first year upon the piece being broken, the team should not be started until about the first of June; not if practicable should it be continued longer than about six weeks. And I believe it is universally admitted that land broken in June decays much faster and a better crop may be observed even for several years than on land broken much earlier or later.

The two principal reasons for this are that the grass is at this time growing with full vigor and the land is then as dry as at any other season of the year. It must be borne in mind, however, that these observations will only apply to our ordinary seasons. For it sometimes happens that June is a very wet month, as in 1833, when I am informed that land broken in August, which was a dry month, proved much better than that broken in June.

Sweet Corn Pudding

3 large ears of raw sweet corn
3 cups milk
4 eggs
1/2 cup cornstarch
1/4 cup sugar

Editor's note:

This dish provides a wonderful example of the steps needed to recreate early recipes. The original recipe called for 3 ears of sweet corn, 6 cups milk, 2 eggs and a spoon of sugar. The directions called to bake 2 or 3 hours and eat hot with butter. Although it looked unlikely, I did try it. Of course the custard didn't set up.

My next thoughts were that sweet corn has become much less starchy in the 160 years since this recipe was first printed. The amount of starch in the scraped corn would impact the thickening of the milk, so I called the Horticulture Department at Iowa State University and discussed with professor Hank Tabor how much I should adjust. We arrived at a formula, and I added the cornstarch as an ingredient to make up for the diminished natural starch. I tried that. It still didn't set up the way I would have liked. So I reduced the milk and added the additional eggs. Now I am pleased with the way this dish tastes and looks. It is best made when the corn is freshest, in July and August.

I hope you enjoy it too.

Preheat the oven to 325 degrees F. The first step in making this delicate pudding is to get the corn kernel off the cob properly. Just like old-fashioned creamed corn, you do not want the tough skin of the kernels. So, run a sharp knife down each row of kernels to split them open. Then take the back of a heavy knife and press it against the cob and push out the creamy insides of each kernel, leaving the skins on the cob. This can be very messy, the corn will want to spray all over, I suggest holding the cob inside a very deep kettle. Combine the cornstarch and sugar. Add them to the corn along with the milk and eggs. Mix well and pour it into a lightly greased casserole dish. Bake until the pudding is firm and just set. Test by putting a knife into the center of the pudding. It should come out nearly clean, with just the slightest bit of the pudding sticking to it. Depending upon the size and depth of your casserole, this could take between an hour to two hours. The corn pudding can be reheated, so I suggest making it ahead.

French Mode of Cooking Tomatoes

August 18, 1883
There will be less loud dressing of the hair hereafter. Bangs are going out of fashion

10 or 12 tomatoes cut in quarters
4 sliced onions
Parsley and thyme to taste
1 clove
1/4 pound butter

Cook 3/4 of an hour, stirring from time to time to keep from sticking. Strain though a colander. As the original recipe said, "serve with mutton chops or beefsteak."

Tomato Tarts

Editor's note:

If you don't have a favorite pie crust recipe, the raised crust for chicken pie in the meat chapter works well.

Crust for a 9-inch bottom crust
6 to 8 plum-type tomatoes
2 tablespoons brown sugar
1 tablespoon cinnamon

Preheat the oven to 425 degrees F. Roll the pie crust out to a 10-inch circle and place on a lightly greased cookie sheet. Roll the outside 1 inch of crust to form a slightly raised edge. Place the tomatoes in slightly overlapping in concentric circles around the crust. Mix the brown sugar and cinnamon and dust over the top of the tomatoes. Bake until the crust is done and the tomatoes are tender and lightly glazed, about 20 minutes.

Tomatoes

This vegetable not only acts as a tonic, but also makes a most delicious diet. They are excellent in soups and the modes in which they are cooked are various. Tomatoes are "good any way you fix 'em." The way in which I prefer them is to slice up in a pan and fry them with fresh meat; or rather, after the meat has been taken out. They make an excellent sauce, a good preserve and a delightful catsup.

Imagine yourself for a minute (now don't get vexed) seated at the table with a nice venison steak, hot upon the chafing dish, smiling with the fumes of tomato catsup! Whew! Pardon me all ye aldermen and epicures, for this exciting your alimentary powers without the means of allaying such irritation.

NOVEMBER 8, 1846

Corn and Beans

An amount sufficient for a family of six or seven.

1/2 pound salt pork (ham or bacon)
3 quarts cold water
2 dozen ears sweet corn
1 quart shelled fresh lima beans
5 or 6 tablespoons butter

Cut the kernels from their cobs and set aside. Boil the now kernel-less cobs with the salt pork in the 2 quarts of water for about 1/2 hour. Remove the cobs and discard. Cut the meat into small pieces and return to the water. Add the lima beans and cook 20 minutes, until almost tender. Add the corn kernels and cook until they are tender, 5 to 10 minutes. Stir in 5 or 6 tablespoons butter.

Cooked Cucumbers

Of their healthfulness thus cooked there can be no question, and of the palatableness, it is only necessary that you try them to say with us that they are exquisite.

Peel and cut the cucumbers into slices 1/4 inch thick. Cut them slightly on the diagonal, rather than into small circular slices or unmanageable lengthwise ones. Dust both sides with corn meal. Melt 3 tablespoons butter in a frying pan. Add the cucumber slices and cook until they are tender and the cornmeal coating is lightly browned. Drain briefly on paper towels.

Egg Plant

Editor's note:

The original recipe did not specify herbs or spices other than the pepper. I've suggested the nutmeg as being typical of the era. However, you could substitute chopped fresh basil, oregano or sage.

1 large egg plant
3 tablespoons dry breadcrumbs
1/2 teaspoon pepper
1/4 teaspoon nutmeg
2 tablespoons butter, melted
1/2 cup milk
3 eggs, well beaten

Peel the eggplant and cut into strips, about 1/2 by 1/2 inch and as long as the eggplant was wide. Gently simmer these slices until tender. Drain well, and pat dry. Combine the pepper, breadcrumbs and nutmeg. Toss the eggplant slices in this mixture and place in a large frying pan with the melted butter. Lightly brown the coating. Combine the milk and eggs; pour over the eggplant and stir until the eggs are set.

Cucumber Sauce

2 or 3 small whole dill pickles, minced
Grated peel of 1 lemon
1/8 teaspoon pepper
2 tablespoons flour
1 cup vegetable broth
2 tablespoons good cream or brown gravy

Mix the minced pickles with the lemon peel, pepper and flour in a small pan. Stir in the vegetable broth and cook over medium heat until the sauce is thickened. Stir in the cream and serve.

Cabbage/Cole Slaw

1/2 head finely shaved cabbage
1/3 cup butter
1/2 teaspoon pepper
1/2 cup vinegar
Salt and pepper

Editor's note:

There are dozens of recipes for hot and cold cabbage slaws in *Prairie Farmer* over the years. One very similar to this recipe ran in January 1852, with the suggestion that the cabbage be boiled for an hour and a half to two hours.

Combine all ingredients in a large frying pan. Cook over medium heat about 5 minutes until the cabbage is wilted. Turn into dish and serve.

Cole slaw

Cut a hard white head of cabbage in two. Shave one half as finely as possible and put it into a stew pan with a bit of butter the size of an egg, one small teaspoon salt and nearly as much pepper. Add to it a wine glass of vinegar. Cover the stew pan and set it over a gentle heat for five minutes.

Breaking the Prairie

To the Prairie Farmer Editor:

We have had a hard frost even to freezing the ground this morning. You wish to know something about breaking the prairie, the depth of plowing &c.

I broke up 7 acres of prairie in September 1840. One acre I broke about 8 inches deep; 6 acres I broke 4 inches deep. The land lay in this state until the spring of 1841; the furrows lay flat on the land that was plowed 4 inches deep, and the furrows of that which was plowed 6 inches deep stood nearly on edge.

I planted potatoes on three-fourths of the acre that was broken the deepest, from which I got only 40 bushels; the potatoes were of a fair size, the English white ones. We had but little rain, which I believe to be the cause of the failure of the potatoes. Three-fourths of an acre I harrowed with a harrow that had wooden teeth, so as not to turn the sod back again, and sowed 1 bushel of the common pea from which I only harvested 3 bushels of peas.

Drought is supposed to be the cause of so great a failure. Three fourths of an acre I harrowed the same as for the peas and sowed one bushel of barley, from which I got 15 bushels, being smutty barley; the drought is supposed to be the cause of the failure. Two acres I worked the same as above described, and sowed 4 bushels of oats on the ground; the oats grew finely and large, but the dry weather came on about the time the grain was forming and there was more straw than anything else.

If the oats have been well threshed, I believe I should have got 40 bushels; but they were threshed on the ground by cattle, so I believe I lost half. I got 20 bushels of oats. Two acres I planted with corn, the corn grew finely until it began to set for ears and silk, when the drought came on and my corn dried up so that I got only abut 20 bushels. We will bear in mind this is the first crop on top of the sod and a most unfavorable season of drought.

—P. Prescot

Cucumber Salad

2 to 4 cucumbers
1 teaspoon salt
10 green onions
3/4 cup vinegar
Juice of half a lemon (2-3 tablespoons)
1/8 teaspoon ground cayenne pepper
1/8 teaspoon ground ginger

Pare the cucumber, cut in half and remove the seeds. Chop into about a 1/2-inch dice. Place in a nonreactive bowl and mix with the salt. Let stand for at least 1 hour. You may keep them salted down for about 4 hours at the most. Drain off the accumulated juices and rinse well under cold water. Peel and slice the green onions into very thin rings and add to the cucumbers. In a small saucepan, mix the vinegar, lemon juice, cayenne pepper and ginger. Heat to boiling and pour over the vegetables. Let stand for at least three hours before serving. Overnight is better. Store in a covered container in the refrigerator. It should keep at least a week.

APRIL 1860

Winter Salad

Editor's note:

Today we seldom see poetry about food. *Prairie Farmer* editors often printed poems that dramatized the relationship between people and food. You'll find several of them throughout this book. This poem gives a recipe for a vinegar and oil salad dressing in verse.

Two large potatoes through the kitchen sieve
unwanted softness to the salad give
of mordant mustard add a single spoon.

Distrust the condiment that bites so soon
but drain it not thou man of herbs a fault
to add a double quantity of salt.

Three times the spoon with oil of lucas crown
and once with vinegar procured from town.
True flavor needs it and your poet begs
the pounded yellow of two well boiled eggs.

Let onion atoms lurk within the bowl
and scarce suspected animate the whole.

And lastly on the flavored compound toss,
a magic teaspoon of anchovy sauce.

Then though the green turtle fall, tho' the
venison's tough and ham and turkey are not
boiled enough, serenely full the epicure may say,
Fate cannot harm me I have dined today.

How to Cook Vegetables and Other Garden 'Sass'

There is not a branch of cookery apparently so simple, yet requiring so much care and judgment as the preparation of summer vegetables; no articles of food more subject to abuse than they and none that become unpalatable and tremendously indigestible from ill treatment.

Now that summer is in reality begun, it is of the utmost importance that the diet should be in accordance with the season. The appetite craves cooling food and pleasing flavors, as in winter the desire was for richer and more carbonaceous articles.

While fruits and vegetables are not in themselves sufficient to satisfy hunger and repair the waste of tissue, many of them are rich in strength-giving qualities and possess properties that are especially beneficial to the system.

Very early vegetables are generally unwholesome for they have been either shriveled and wilted by being brought from a distance, or have been forced into unnatural forwardness, and hence are wholly lacking in nutritive qualities and are comparatively tasteless.

Vegetables are in perfection when in full season, and will require much less time for cooking while fresh than after being kept. When wilted they are wholly worthless, for much of their goodness lies in their natural moisture, and the evaporation of this fluid renders them not only unpleasant to the eye, but unwholesome and unpalatable as well.

Let your vegetables then be perfectly fresh and of medium size. Wash and cleanse them well, and lay cabbage, cauliflower and spinach into cold salt water for an hour before cooking them. Nearly all vegetables should be put into boiling water and with but few exceptions the water should be salted. One of these is green corn; salt will render it hard and tasteless.

Those that should look green when done must be left uncovered. Those that should look white must be boiled in a mixture of milk and water. The more rapidly they cook the better they will be and should never be allowed to stop boiling after they once begin until they are done, when they should be dished immediately, well drained and served hot. If allowed to cook too long, they will lose both color and flavor. If not boiled tender they will be not only tasteless but also highly indigestible.

Summing up the whole matter, "When they are good they are very, very good, and when they are bad they are horrid."

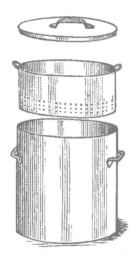

To Prepare:

Raw Tomatoes

Choose firm, smooth ripe fruit, lay it in a cool place until wanted, then pare with a very sharp knife, without scalding. Slice evenly and lay carefully in a glass dish, sprinkle with salt and pepper and scatter bits of ice over the surface. In this manner, each person can suit their individual taste in regard to oil, vinegar and sugar.

Many persons prefer to serve with tomatoes a dressing of oil and mustard mixed until thick to which is added sugar and vinegar. Still others enjoy eating them with cream and sugar. However they are seasoned, it is much better to lay ice over them adding the dressing after they are dished.

Stuffed Tomatoes

Cut a thin slice from the upper part of a smooth, ripe tomato. Do not peel. Take out all of the inside and chop it first. Fry a very little chopped onion, add some butter and when it is turning yellow add the chopped tomato and a few fine bread crumbs. Stir it well. Season with salt, pepper and a little chopped parsley. Both this and the onion can be omitted if not liked. Sim-

mer a minute and fill the tomato with the mixture. Place in a pan; fit each top on its own tomato and bake for an hour or until a light brown.

Scalloped Tomatoes

Peel ripe tomatoes and slice, not too thin. Put a layer in the bottom of a buttered pudding dish. Sprinkle well with fine bread crumbs, pepper, salt, a little sugar and a few bits of butter. Add another layer of tomatoes, and the crumbs etc. as before. Fill the dish almost full and season the top layer of tomatoes. Put bread crumbs over all and bake for an hour. Cover the dish for half the time; then remove the cover and let it brown.

Green Peas

Keep them free from dust and leaves while you shell them so they will not have to be washed. Put them into boiling water in which is some salt and a small lump of sugar. Have only sufficient water to cover them well and put no lid on the saucepan. Boil for 20 minutes; drain well and pour over them some sweet cream in which is melted a little butter. Sprinkle with pepper and serve hot. If the pods are very fresh and green, wash a few of them and put over the top of the peas while they are boiling; it improves the flavor wonderfully. A sprig of mint is often boiled with peas.

String Beans

Choose young beans. Break off top and bottom and string carefully. Cut, slanting into pieces an inch long. Unless quite young, they will need to boil longer. Cook until tender, and serve in the same manner, or substitute rich milk for the cream and stir in through them a lump of butter which has been well rolled in flour. Let all come to a boil before serving. A piece of bacon may be boiled with them.

Beets

Wash, but do not cut. Boil until tender, according to their size. Skin and slice them into a hot dish. Mix 1 tablespoon of butter, 1 of vinegar, a little pepper and salt. Bring to a boil and pour over the beets and serve them hot.

Lima Beans

Lay them in cold water for one hour. Put into plenty of boiling water. Salt slightly and cook until tender. Drain and when dished, stir in a good lump of butter and a little chopped parsley through them.

Summer Squash

Unless very young, pare them and take out the seeds. Cut in pieces and boil in salted water until tender. Press out the water and mash smooth. Season with butter, pepper and salt and a tablespoon of cream. Put into a frying pan and let simmer for 10 minutes or longer.

Spinach

Wash through three waters and leave for half an hour in water slightly salted. Put it into boiling water with a little salt. Put it well under and boil very rapidly for about 10 minutes — no longer. Drain and press out every bit of water Place on a dish and score crosswise into squares, garnish with slices of hard boiled egg or serve with it eggs poached and laid on buttered toast.

Asparagus

Scrape the lower part of the stalks and tie them in small bunches with strips of muslin. Put into boiling water only enough to cover them, with a little salt, and boil for 20 minutes or one half hour. Do not cover the saucepan. Dip some slices of toast in the asparagus water, butter them and arrange on a hot platter. On this lay the asparagus, remove the muslin, sprinkle with pepper and pour some melted butter over all.

<hr>

JANUARY 30, 1886

Cooking Potatoes for Supper

In this cold weather, we are fond of having potatoes cooked for supper, and I have a very nice, relishable and quickly cooked dish made thus.

Pare and slice the potatoes for frying. Have some scalding milk in a double boiler. Season it with salt and butter and pepper if liked; put in the potatoes and let them cook just long enough

to get thoroughly soft. A very little chopped parsley in the gravy improves it.

We think these are better than fried potatoes and they are certainly more digestible and more easily prepared if one is busy.

—Mrs. Knight

How to Cook Carrots

I cut the carrots into thin slices and fry in butter or lard very slowly. When tender, I pour over them a little cream. Salt and pepper and serve hot. This is the only way our family will eat them, and think myself that they are very nice.

—Mrs. A. Lundstrum, Marshall County, Iowa

AUGUST 28, 1886

A Nice Tomato Salad

To the various dishes of tomatoes in last week's talk, I will add another pretty one for a lunch or tea dish. Select ripe tomatoes of medium size, skin them and leave whole. Then cool an hour or two in the refrigerator.

When wanted, lay around each on a platter the crisp inner leaves of lettuce. Serve a tomato with the lettuce under it to each person. Have a dressing to pass with it made thus: Stir together until smooth a tablespoon of olive oil or the same of melted butter, as much sugar and mustard with a teaspoonful of salt. Then add the yolks of three eggs, well beaten, 1 cup of vinegar and lastly the same amount of milk.

Put it on to cook in a double boiler and let it remain until it thickens like custard. Stir until it is cooled.

—Mrs. Raikes

January 26, 1867
Skillful cooking is as readily discovered in a nicely baked potato or a respectable johnny cake as in a nut brown sirloin or a brace of canvas-back ducks.

Houseflies in Warm Weather

Flies during this hot summer weather are a great annoyance to housekeepers and others in every vicinity. For their benefit, we print the following, going the rounds of our exchanges. It is a simple and cheap remedy and contains nothing poisonous, as many of the articles recommended for the destruction of the troublesome insects do.

Houseflies may be effectively destroyed by taking half a spoonful of black pepper in powder, a tablespoon of brown sugar and one teaspoon of cream. Mix them well together and place them in a room where the flies are troublesome. They will soon disappear.

Mashed Potato Salad

This will make a very relishable salad to eat with cold meats.

Editor's note:

Although this recipe calls for mashed potatoes, I think the author intended to have minced cooked potatoes. If you look at an old-fashioned potato masher, it would be easy to use it to make minced potatoes about the same size as the chopped cabbage. A smoothly mashed or instant-style potato would not work.

2 cups mashed potatoes
1 cup chopped cabbage
1 tablespoon minced onion
2 hard-boiled egg yolks, chopped

For the dressing:
1 tablespoon dry mustard
1 tablespoon sugar
1 tablespoon flour
Pinch salt
1/8 teaspoon white pepper
1 egg
1/2 cup vinegar

Combine the dry dressing ingredients in a small pot. In a small mixing cup, beat the egg lightly and whip in the vinegar. Stir this into the dry ingredients and cook 5 minutes, stirring as it thickens. Pour while hot over the vegetables.

Potato Salad

Boil some new potatoes and let them get cold; then cut them in slices, and arrange them neatly, in some sort of pattern, on a dish, with hard-cooked eggs cut into slices, slices of beet-root stamped out into shapes, and olives. The dish should be slightly rubbed with a shallot.

Make a sauce with two parts oil and one (part) tarragon vinegar; pepper and salt, a little tarragon, some capers, chervil, parsley, and a few leaves of thyme, all finely minced; beat the sauce well together, pour over the salad and serve.

Boston Baked Beans

We preserve our old New England custom of having baked beans for breakfast on Sunday morning, and we think it could hardly be improved upon.

After carefully picking over and washing the beans, I put them on the fire in cold water boil a few minuets then pour off the water and put them into a gallon bean pot. To a quart of beans, take 1 pound of salt pork, scrape and score the rind and place it on top of the beans.

In a cup, mix 1 teaspoonful each of made mustard, ginger and baking soda and 1 tablespoon molasses. Add boiling water to dissolve the whole. Pour it over the beans and fill with cold water to within an inch or two of the top.

Set it in the oven and bake three or four hours or until the beans are thoroughly soft. I leave it in the oven on Saturday night and it is ready to warm quickly in the morning.

—Mrs. Raikes

Rocky Point Potatoes

Editor's note:

Dinner leftovers frequently appeared at the breakfast table. Hearty hashes of meat and potatos formed the foundation for the morning's farm work. This recipe is like a potato pancake.

Baked potatoes left over from dinner are fine for breakfast next morning. Chop quite fine, and put in a spider with a little cream or milk, salt and butter the size of an egg, warm quickly.

Sliced Potato Salad

3 or 4 cooked red potatoes, cut into slices
1/2 cup diced onion
Salt and pepper to taste

For the dressing:
1/2 teaspoon dry mustard
1/4 teaspoon sugar
1 well-beaten egg
1/2 cup vinegar

Mix the dressing ingredients; cook over medium heat until thickened. Pour the hot dressing over the potatoes and onions.

AUGUST 26, 1888

Thickened Tomatoes

I always save all crumbs and pieces of bread. When I have a few stewed tomatoes left over and bread is scarce just before baking, I make a dish, which I call thickened tomatoes. The children are very fond of it and will make a hearty meal entirely of it.

To make it, I take a quart of milk into a bright pan on the stove to heat. When hot, I put in 2 cups of bread broken into bits, let it boil until the bread is light and soft and then season with salt, pepper and a little piece of butter. Add the cold tomatoes of which I like to have nearly a cup. Stir well and when it boils again, serve.
—Mrs. Gray

May 19, 1859
The man who would shine in converstion must possess original ideas and strong sympathies — be able both to communicate and to listen

CHAPTER FIVE

Preserves

Everything has a season and the writers and readers of *Prairie Farmer* knew how to make the most of the seasonal bounty and prepare for scarcity. Preserving food of all kinds, not just putting up jams and jellies, is a significant part of the homemaking columns and letters, especially those written during the first three decades from 1841 to just after the Civil War.

As the days of preserving and canning fruits draw nigh, every one is anxiously asking for the best methods, each telling their experience of last year: how much was lost and how much saved and wondering how it could be. "They thought they did all alike and yet they did not keep."
August 19, 1858

No prairie farm lunch, dinner or tea was complete without home-made pickles, catsup, jams and jellies to "lend relish to the meal." Pumpkins and pears, in addition to tomatoes and cucumbers, were transformed with solutions of vinegar, sugar and spices. Reading through the pages of the magazine, it almost seems that from late summer through the fall, if produce came into the kitchen, it was pickled, preserved or made into catsup.

Recipes were exchanged in the magazine columns for types of "meat pickle," which was achieved by putting beef or pork down in salt and spice solutions in barrels to keep for months. The writings include a very lively discussion among readers regarding various methods for keeping eggs over the winter when the hens are not laying. Various styles of icehouses and cold cellars are illustrated and described. We've included some of those columns.

Most of these combinations have disappeared from cookbooks in the more than 100 years since they were published in *Prairie Farmer*. I think they are well worth rediscovering. Some of these recipes are written for the experienced cook, but many of them can be prepared easily and in small quantities. Try the apple catsup, spiced jelly or French mustard and you will see how easy it can be to have a "store sauce" in your pantry to make a delicious difference to your meals.

To Preserve Fruit

From an exchanged newspaper:

Twenty nine years ago Betty Winal, then residing at Tarleton, bottled a quantity of white currants in their green state, being then in the 33rd year of her age. Having kept them some time in a state of preservation, William (her husband) and she agreed that they should be kept while they both lived and that they should be made into pies at the funeral of the one of them who should die first.

The wife departed this life on the second of this month and was interred at St. Peter's Church, Preston, on the fourth — the family having removed to Dawson Street, Preston. Their mutual pledge was fulfilled and the pies made out of these currants were served out, after returning from the church, every attendant taking a slice. Though the currants had kept 29 years, they were as fresh as if just taken from the trees. Any other fruit may be preserved in this way by expelling the air and sealing the cork air tight.

Prairie Farmer editor reply:

We have, at many times, put gooseberries in a bottle, clean and dry, without any cold or hot water or any thing else except corking tight and covering the cork with sealing wax and putting into a cellar, had gooseberry pies as fresh at New Year's as though the fruit had just been taken from the bush. We have some now, Dec. 10, in keeping for the first day of 1852.

It may be a matter of curiosity to keep fruit for 29 years, but all practical purposes are answered by keeping six or eight months.

March 17, 1888
Frontier Preserves
One pint of molasses,
sorghum is best, bring it to
a boil, stir into it 2 well-
beaten eggs. Let it boil 10
minutes, and then flavor it
with nutmeg.

Candied Cucumber

10 large cucumbers
Salt
3 cups sugar
1 1/2 cups water

Pare the cucumbers, cut in quarters lengthwise, remove seeds and cut into 1-inch pieces. Cover the cucumbers with salt and ice. Set aside overnight. Rinse and drain. Put in a large kettle and barely cover with fresh water. Bring to a boil. Simmer until transparent. Drain the cucumbers and dry on a sieve. Make a syrup of the sugar and water. Cook 10 minutes. Add the cucumbers and cook gently until tender. Take out; rinse off excess syrup. Put on a rack and place in oven for 2 or 3 days until dry, or put in your food dehydrator.

Cucumber Vinegar

This is excellent for using with salad and cold meat.

2 cups vinegar
5 cucumbers, grated
1 onion
1 shallot
Garlic, to taste
1 teaspoon pepper
1/4 teaspoon cayenne

Mix all ingredients in a nonreactive bowl and cover tightly. Let stand four days in the refrigerator. Strain through a fine filter. Disgard the solids. Store vinegar in the refrigerator.

Use of Watermelons

I will give our mode of using up watermelons. I endeavor every year to raise a good watermelon patch. They are a healthy and delightful fruit, I think. I cultivate the ice rind variety early in May and again towards the close of the month, so that they may come on in succession. When they commence ripening, we commence eating, and use them freely during the hot weather.

When the weather becomes cool in September, we haul a quantity of them to the house, split them open and with a spoon scrape out the pulps into a cullender and strain the water into vessels. We boil it in iron vessels down to a syrup.

Then put the syrup into a brass kettle and put in apples or peaches, like making apple butter, and boil slowly until the fruit is well cooked. Then spice to taste, and you have something that most of people will prefer to apple butter or any kind of preserves.

Or the syrup may be boiled without fruit, down to molasses, which will be found to be as fine as the best sugar house molasses. We have made of a fall, as much as 10 gallons of the apple butter, if I may so call it, and molasses, which has kept until May in fine condition.

—William Vawter, Hannival, Mo.

Recipe for Tomato Figs

Pour boiling water over the tomatoes in order to remove the skin; then weigh them and place in a stone jar with the same amount of sugar as tomatoes. Let them stand two days, and then pour off the syrup. Boil and skim it until no scum rises.

Pour this syrup over the tomatoes and let them stand two days as before; then boil them and skim again. After the third time, they are fit to dry if the weather is good. If not, let them stand in the syrup until drying weather then place them on large earthen dishes or plates and put them in the sun to dry, which will take about a week, after which pack them down in small wooden boxes with fine white sugar between every layer.

Tomatoes prepared in this way will keep for years. A few apples cut up and boiled in the remainder of the syrup, make a nice sauce.

Wild Plums

Editor's note:

The recipes on these two pages highlight the adaptive thinking of pioneer cooks. According to many of the period diaries, early prairie settlers found the river banks lined with wild currants and plum trees.

Often these native plants were transplanted to cabin yards where the fruit was made into a variety of jams, jellies, pickles and sauces.

Tomatoes and pumpkins also provided important and adaptable substitute for apples, until orchards were established.

The wild plum makes excellent jelly. Scald them a few minutes in weak saleratus water to remove the bitterness from the skins. Pour that off and add pure water; boil till very tender then strain; add an equal part of sugar and boil gently for about 15 minutes.

A good deal of the pulp of the plum is left, which, if pressed through a colander and added to half its quantity of sugar, makes a good marmalade. Boil gently and stir till done. The wild plum makes excellent pickles.

JANUARY 6, 1859

Pumpkin Butter

One regular-size can of pumpkin
1/2 cup molasses
1/4 cup vinegar
1/4 teaspoon allspice
1/8 teaspoon cinnamon

Combine all ingredients in a medium-sized saucepan. Cook over very low heat until the mixture has thickened. You will need to stir this frequently to keep from scorching. Put in a jar and store in the refrigerator for up to three weeks.

Preserved Cucumbers

For each 16 cucumbers:
1 pound sugar
1 cup water

Peel and seed the cucumbers; cut into thin slices. Sprinkle generously with salt and set in the regfrigerator over night.

In the morning, drain and rinse the cucumbers. Combine the sugar and water. Add the cucumbers and boil slowly until they are clear. Remove the cucumbers. Boil down the syrup until thick. Add juice of 2 lemons and 2 slices of ginger root. Pour over cucumbers and seal in sterilized jars.

The Last of the Pickles

*Tis the last of the pickles
Left souring alone: All its little companions
Are eaten and gone.
No kindred cucumber,
No mango is nigh,
To respond to the last pickle's
Sorrowful sigh.*

*I'll not leave thee, thou lonely one,
To pine in the jar,
While thy kinfolk are scattered
In regions afar.
Thus kindly I see thee,
And eat thee down fast.
With mournful reflection
That thou are the last.*

*So soon may I follow,
When friends day by day,
From Creation's vast pickle jar
Vanish away
Oh, who would be left
When the loved one's have flown
Mid life's waste of vinegar,
Floating alone.*

Tomato Catsup

2 quarts peeled and seeded fresh tomatoes
(or 1 large commercial can of tomatoes)
2 tablespoons salt
3 ounces ground cloves
2 ounces black pepper
2 teaspoons grated nutmeg
1/2 teaspoon cayenne pepper
(more or less to taste)
2 cups cider vinegar

Chop the tomatoes into medium-sized chunks and mix them with the salt. Set aside in a cool place (or refrigerate) overnight. Drain off the accumulated juices and reserve for another purpose. Process the tomatoes in a food processor or blender. Stir in the spices and vinegar. Cook until thick over medium heat, stirring frequently so the mixture doesn't burn. Put in sterilized jars and process, or keep in the refrigerator.

OCTOBER 27, 1866

Chili Sauce

Editor's note:

These two recipes are favorites in our family. We now find commercial ketchup too salty and otherwise bland. The Chili Sauce has scores of uses — as a condiment, or as a base for vegetable soup with a bit of leftover roast beef and water to make the stock, mixed with ground beef for meatloaf, or thickened with a bit of honey for a barbecue sauce for chicken.

2 quarts ripe tomatoes
1 large onion
6 small green peppers
1 cup sugar
2 1/2 cups vinegar
2 teaspoons salt
1 teaspoon each ground allspice, cloves, cinnamon, ginger, mace and nutmeg

Peel and seed the tomatoes, peel and chop the onion, seed the peppers. Use a food processor, blender or food grinder to chop the vegetables into very small pieces, about 1/4 of an inch. But do not over-process. You do want recognizable pieces, not mush. Combine the vegetables with the remaining ingredients in a large kettle. Bring to a boil, reduce heat and simmer until the onions look transparent and the mixture has thickened. Put into sterilized jars and store in the refrigerator, or you may process in a hot-water bath.

An Ice House Dialogue

ICE HOUSE.

I wish to say to the members of the club that now is the time to have an ice house built. I am convinced by my summer's experience that it is one of the most economical institutions on a farm. We built one last fall, and I am sure we have saved all it cost us this summer, and it has saved me any amount of trouble. Ice is a luxury that costs a farmer little money or time.

—Mrs. Gardner

Will Mrs. Gardner tell us how her ice house was built? During some of the warm muggy weather of last summer, when it was almost an impossibility to keep anything eatable more than 24 hours, I determined to have ice in some way for another summer.

—Mrs. Montgomery

Our ice house cost about $30. It is built on the north side of the house on a level piece of ground. The floor is covered with cheap boarding, spaces being left between the boards for drainage. Stout posts are placed at each corner the two in the front being 2 feet higher than those in the back, which gives a sharp slant to the roof. Rough boards are nailed all around the posts, inside and out. The space between the boards is filled with sawdust, which also covers the floor to a depth of 10 inches. The roof is of boards covered with slabs. Our ice house is about 12 feet square. For filling it, Mr. Gardner chooses very cold days. He tries to have the ice cut in as large blocks as convenient, selecting clear solid ice. These blocks are left exposed to the air for an hour or two after they are lifted from the water before being packed. After sufficient ice is stored, sawdust to the depth of 2 feet is covered over it. When using ice, care is taken to replace the covering after a piece is removed.

—Mrs. Gardner

Prepared Table Mustard

Few housekeepers know how easily and cheaply they can prepare table mustard much superior to the vile stuff generally used. All that is necessary is to take say a tablespoon of ground mustard (the genuine Durham purchased at drug stores is best); add to it a pinch of salt, pepper and ginger and half a teaspoon of sugar, and finally mix with sufficient vinegar to give it the right consistency. By following this suggestion, one may always have on the table nice yellow mustard instead of that disgusting black paste so frequently met with.

—Pharakeus

French Mustard

From the Scientific American
One of the most refreshing condiments which has ever been invented is known as French mustard. It is equally good with fish, flesh or fowl and wonderfully helps bachelors' bread and cheese (Betty says they don't deserve anything better) to go down savorily. The following recipe is an excellent way to make it. Put the mixture into small pots, with a teaspoon of vinegar on the top. Cork it well down, as its flavor improves by age. It may be kept a month or six weeks before it is brought to the table. No less than 5 tons of mustard so prepared are imported every year from France to England, and a large amount is annually imported and consumed in this city. Why not make it at home?

1 can dry mustard
1 tablespoon each dried parsley, tarragon, chervil and celery seeds
(You may substitute fresh herbs, and use 3 tablespoons each, minced.)
1 or 2 shallots, minced
1 anchovy or 1/2 teaspoon salt
2 tablespoons honey
2 tablespoons vinegar
1/4 cups water (more or less)

Combine the mustard, herbs, shallot and anchovy (or salt) in a food processor or blender. Process until well mixed. Add the honey and vinegar and slowly begin adding the water, processing until the mixture is smooth and of a desired consistency. Store in the refrigerator for a week or two.

Tomato Marmalade

Gather full-grown tomatoes while quite green. Take out the stems and stew them quite soft, then rub them through a sieve, put the pulp over the fire, season highly with pepper, salt and powdered cloves and let it stew until quite thick. The article will keep well and is excellent for seasoning gravies.

Apple Catsup

I was lamenting that our tomatoes were not ripening so that I could make catsup. Mr. Rodney's sister who is visiting us said that apples make a nice catsup and proposed to help me make some.

—*Mrs. Rodney*

7 cups apple pulp
from 7 to 10 fresh apples or more
(or 2 large, 32-ounce, jars applesauce)
1 1/2 cups sugar
1 teaspoon dry mustard
1 teaspoon pepper
1 teaspoon ground cloves
1 teaspoon cinnamon
1 teaspoon ground ginger
2 medium onions, chopped fine
4 cups vinegar

If you are using fresh apples, peel and core them and process in a food processor or blender. If you are using the applesauce, line a sieve with coffee filters and drain the excess liquid from the applesauce for 30 minutes. Combine all ingredients in a large pot. Simmer, stirring frequently, until the onions are transparent and the mixture has thickened. Set aside to cool and then process in a blender until smooth. Put in sterilized jars and store in the refrigerator or you may process in a hot-water bath.

Spiced Jelly

1 large jar apple jelly
1/4 teaspoon ginger
1/4 teaspoon cinnamon
1/8 teaspoon cloves
1/8 teaspoon allspice

Melt the jelly slowly in a medium saucepan. Add the spices and continue to cook over very low heat, stirring frequently until the spices are blended into the jelly. Let cool slightly and pour the jelly back in the jar. Stir from time to time to assure the spices don't sink to the bottom as the jelly re-solidifies.

Picked Onions

October is the proper month for making these pickles. —Marie Mignonette

Editor's note:

The original recipe begins with "small white onions the size of hickory nuts" boiling, peeling and then cooking until tender. You may certainly begin with fresh onions, but I think the ones already cooked work just fine.

1 jar peeled small white onions
1 cup vinegar
1 teaspoon mustard seed
1/2 teaspoon mace
1/4 teaspoon cayenne pepper
or 2 or 3 hot peppers

Combine the vinegar, mustard seed, mace and pepper in a small pan. Drain the onions and add them to the vinegar. Bring to a boil, lower the heat and simmer for 10 minutes. Cool and put back in the jar. Allow to mellow in the refrigerator for 2 or 3 days before eating; will keep in the refrigerator for a couple of weeks.

OCTOBER 16, 1875

Cucumber Catsup

3 large cucumbers, peeled, seeded, and grated
1 onion, peeled and minced
1 tablespoon salt
2 1/2 teaspoons black pepper
1 1/2 cups white vinegar

Mix the cucumbers and onions with salt. Put the vegetables into a cheesecloth-lined colander and let stand one hour. Pour out drained juices and gently squeeze the vegetable mixture until dry. If you want to reduce the salt content, you may rinse off the vegetable mixture before you squeeze it dry. Mix the vegetables, vinegar, and pepper in a heavy stockpot. Cook gently until the mixture is hot and has turned somewhat yellow. Cool and then carefully process in a food processor or blender until smooth. Return to the heavy pot and simmer until thick, stirring to prevent sticking as it reduces and thickens. Pour into clean, sterilized jars and seal. Keeps for a month or two in the refrigerator.

A Dialogue on Economy

Editor's note:

This exchange of letters between Mrs. Clark and Mrs. Franklin is a fine example of how *Prairie Farmer* provided a forum for readers to exchange ideas on issues of the time.

Mrs. Clark asks:

I want to ask your opinion about furnishing my table, Mrs. Franklin. Mr. Clark's brother is boarding with us now and I am at my wits' end to provide a suitable variety with eggs and butter so high and scarce. And meat, too; our butcher's bill was positively frightful last month. And much of the time we only had meat once a day. We have been accustomed on the farm to our own butter, eggs and milk, with plenty of ham, sausage and lard always on hand; but Mr. Clark thinks pork very unhealthy. We have a good supply of vegetables, apples and canned fruit, but meats, butter and eggs are the problem I cannot solve without spending more that I ought now that times are so hard.

My husband's income is much less than last year and I am anxious to economize, but I positively cannot get along with less than 5 pounds of butter a week with no other shortening for anything else. I have studied the bills of fare in Prairie Farmer for cheap meals and though we do not need to come down to 3 or 5 cents a meal, yet it seems as if there must be a medium.

Mrs. Franklin replies:

We never use swine's flesh in any form either. And when I began housekeeping, I had no idea of fresh beef except in the form or steak or roast; but I soon learned there were other pieces very palatable if properly cooked, and which afford as much nourishment with less outlay.

The next time you buy beef, get a rib piece or some kind of boiled piece 5 pounds of which will probably cost 30 cents. Put it in boiling water well salted and cook until tender. Then place it in the oven half an hour before dinner to brown it over, if you like to do so. If not, bring it to the table just as you take it from the kettle. Make a gravy by thickening some of the broth it was boiled in. Have potatoes, pared and steamed, and mashed turnips and pickles. Set away the kettle in which the meat was boiled and when cold remove every particle of fat; melt it, adding a pinch of soda, strain and set aside.

Next morning, put your kettle over the fire early before breakfast, if possible; add more water and any vegetables you like in soup. Boil until the vegetables mash easily and season to taste. You will probably have soup sufficient for two dinners for your small family. Make two or three pies; for shortening use the fat which you have clarified and strained. Your crust will not be so white and flaky as if made of lard, but very good.

Soup, cold beef sliced, mashed potatoes, beets and pie may be your bill of fare for dinner. Next day soup, some more of the beef, chopped, seasoned, warmed with a little gravy and laid on squares of toasted bread, pickled beets left over from yesterday and put in vinegar overnight, with pie for dessert. If you find you have scraps of cold meat and dry bread or crackers, scallop the meat and have potato soup.

With plenty of vegetables you might occasionally serve a meal without any meat by having potato soup followed by baked beans, scalloped tomatoes and a good dessert. Or bean soup followed by baked potatoes and onions or parsnips.

Small Yellow Tomato Pickles

Use small yellow tomatoes. Prick each tomato several times with a fork or coarse needle. Put them in a dish; cover with boiling water. Let stand 10 minutes. Make a syrup with 3/4 pound sugar to 1 pound tomatoes. Flavor with lemon and ginger root. Drop the tomatoes in and when tender put in jars.

August 25, 1883
"Take care of the useful and the beautiful will take care of itself." This is what the fond and many-time father remarked when he married off his ugliest daughter first.

SEPTEMBER 16, 1888

Watermelon Pickles

Peel the watermelon and soak overnight in weak salt water. Make a syrup with 3/4 pound sugar to 1 pound watermelon. Add 1 sliced lemon. In the morning, scald in weak ginger water. Boil in syrup until tender. Put in jar.

SEPTEMBER 16, 1888

Baked Rhubarb for Sauce

Peel as for pies, but cut in pieces at least 1 inch long and place in an earthen or granite-ware baking dish. To 2 quarts of the rhubarb, allow 1 1/4 cups sugar, sprinkling it over the top. Bake until tender. No water is needed. Any flavoring can be added that is desired, or it is good without anything of the kind.

Cooked in this way, it takes less sugar than when stewed and looks nicer. Some prefer this sauce for pies, instead of filling with the uncooked plant; but it is best to always bake the under-crust first. It is quite rich and tastes much like fruit preserves.

Rhubarb Jelly

An excellent jelly, especially for cake, can be made of this plant. It will not become as stiff as that made of currants, plums, &c. But is more desirable for cake on that account, as it spreads so easily.

Cook as for sauce, using only enough water to keep from burning and, when cool enough, press the juice through a strong but thick muslin bag, not allowing any of the pulp to pass through. Weigh the juice before boiling and allow 3/4

pound of white sugar to each pound of juice. Boil the juice 20 minutes, then add the sugar and cook until it jellies, which can be tested by dipping out a spoonful in a small dish and letting it cool a few minutes.

When it is done, it will be quick thick, although it becomes thicker as it cools completely. If three-quarters of the rhubarb juice and one-fourth of raspberry juice is used, it is hard to tell from pure raspberry jelly.

Chopped Pickles

1/2 bushel green tomatoes (25 pounds)
1 dozen green peppers
2 cabbages
1 ripe cucumber
1/4 cup salt

2 pounds brown sugar
2 tablespoons cinnamon
1 tablespoon ground allspice
1 tablespoon black pepper
1/2 cup dry mustard
2 cups grated horseradish
(If you use the bottled kind, make sure it is not cream style)
1 gallon vinegar

Editor's note:

Finding a good use for green tomatoes is a constant through the years of the *Prairie Farmer*. These end-of-season relishes are a good answer. The combination of the sweet and pungent spices makes an interesting change from the more typical mustard or mixed pickling blends. If you don't have massive quantities of vegetables, try the recipe starting with 6 pounds of green tomatoes and dividing all the other ingredients by four. However, I would use the entire cucumber.

Grind or process all the vegetables into small pieces. Combine in a large pot with 1/4 cup salt. In the morning, drain the vegetables and rinse to remove the excess salt. In a very large stock pot, combine the remaining ingredients. Bring to boiling; carefully add the drained vegetables. When the mixture begins to boil again, lower the temperature and simmer until the vegetables are tender, about 20 to 30 minutes. Bottle in sterilized jars and process in a boiling-water bath.

Green Tomato Pickles

Have two wooden pails full of sliced green tomatoes, sprinkled with salt and left overnight. In the morning, drain well by leaving them awhile in a casket or colander.

Put together 1 teacup full of ground allspice, 1 cup of cinnamon, 1/2 cup of cloves, 1/2 cup of pepper if the berry is used — while a cup if bought readily ground, as it is not strong — 1 box of mustard, 2 pounds sugar, 1 gallon of vinegar and half the drained tomatoes.

Put them over the fire till they come to a boil, skim out then put in the rest of the tomatoes and bring to a boil as before; then pour all in a jar together. They are fit for use immediately, but will keep till next July.

French Pickles

1 colander sliced green tomatoes
1 quart sliced onions
1 colander sliced cucumbers
1/4 cup salt
1/2 ounce celery seed
1/2 ounce allspice berries
1 cup white mustard seed
1/2 cup black peppercorns
1 tablespoon turmeric
1/2 pound brown sugar
2 tablespoons dry mustard
1 gallon vinegar

Combine the vegetables with the salt and set aside overnight in a cool place (or refrigerate) Drain the liquid off and rinse off the salt. In large stockpot combine the spices, sugar, mustard and vinegar. Bring to a boil and carefully add the vegetables. Cook, stirring occasionally until the vegetables are tender. Bottle in sterilized jars and keep in the refrigerator, or process in a boiling-water bath.

Editor's note:

This pickle recipe is spiced similarly to the ones we find in today's cookbooks. In working with these recipes, I was surprised not to find much mention of dill. Certainly dill pickles existed 100 years ago, but the ladies of *Prairie Farmer* didn't write much about them.

Pumpkin Sweet Pickles

4 or 5 cups pumpkin, peeled, seeded and cut
 into thin slices like cucumber pickles

1 quart vinegar
2 pounds sugar
1 teaspoon molasses
1 teaspoon cinnamon
1 teaspoon cloves
1 teaspoon ginger

Combine the vinegar, sugar, molasses and
spices. Bring to a boil, reduce heat and
simmer for 5 minutes. Carefully add the
pumpkin slices and cook, stirring until they
are just tender and transparent. Put in
sterilized jars and keep refrigerated or
process in a boiling water bath.

Editor's note:

These recipes work with any
 kind of fresh pumpkin.

Pumpkin Preserve

Begin with equal amounts of pumpkin and
sweet apples. Peel and cut the pumpkin into
pieces about 1 inch square by 1/2 inch
thick. Also peel the sweet apples and cut
them into slices.

Syrup for each pound of fruit:
1/2 pound sugar
1 sliced lemon
1 teaspoon ginger
1 cup water

Bring the syrup to a boil. Carefully add the
pumpkin and apples. Reduce heat to simmer
and cook for 5 minutes. Let the fruit remain
in the syrup. Refrigerate overnight. The next
day, drain the fruit. Once again, bring the
syrup to a boil; add the fruit. Simmer for
another 5 minutes. Put in sterilized jars.
Store in the refrigerator or process in a
boiling water bath.

Profits from a Corn Crop

From a Macon County farmer:

Lately I read in your paper a statement showing the profits of farming on a farm of 62 acres in Iowa. 1863 must, however, be considered an exceptional year, the fortunate few who escaped the unprecedented August frosts realizing from 300 to 500 percent over ordinary prices for their produce.

Nevertheless, few persons residing in regions where rocks abound have any conception how cheaply and easily crops are raised in our rich prairie regions. I know something of the results of farming in one of the most fertile valleys of Pennsylvania where farming land is worth $75 to $150 an acre, and I think a majority owning farms of 100 acres upwards — after a lifetime of more downright hard work than is performed in any other part of the world — are no richer than when they commenced. Wealth would reward the same capital and labor in the West.

I bought land of the Illinois Central Railroad Co. in 1861, improved and leased it at two dollars and fifty cents cash per acre, which yields me at least 18 percent net on the investment. It would pay still better on the shares — one-third of cultivated crops and one-half of hay to the landlord. The increase in the value of property besides would be a moderate estimate of ten percent.

Mr. Sterrett of our county, on his first arrival here some years, ago kept accounts of his crops, the expense of labor, results &c. and I annex his statement of a corn crop on a 90-acre field. The old one-horse plow was used in cultivating. The result per acre is one that Mr. S., with the experience acquired since, would not be satisfied with. Several good farmers to whom I showed this account deemed the summary about right. Labor is at present higher, but the improved cultivators

&c. more than counterbalance that.

Plowing: 33 days at $2 day	$66.00
Planting: 5 1/2 days	$14.00
Harrowing: 15 days	$30.00
Cultivating: 60 days	$60.00
Cribbing: 4,400 bushels	$88.00
Rent per acre: $2	$180.00
Total	**$438.00**

Product: 4,400 bushels
Cost: less than 10 cents per bushel

I am informed that for many years before the war, corn commanded at least 25 cents per bushel at some period during each year in this county. And those who paid that price generally made a big profit in other markets. At that price and the moderate estimate of 50 bushels to the acre, the results would be as follows:

Gross receipts for one acre of corn	$12.50
Deduct labor, rent &c. as above, 10 cents per bushel	$5.00
Deduct shelling, teaming &c. 5 cents per bushel	$2.50
Net	$5.00

Thus the farmer, after being paid his rent and fair wages for himself or his hands, had a margin of $5 per acre for his land.

With us, industry among farmers is well rewarded. But here, as in all regions favored by nature, is a class who take every excuse to loaf, spend half their time and all their cash in town, mostly returning boozy, buttonholing all whom they can get to stand and deliver small talk by the hour, an excuse for idleness. Always hard up, they haul their crops to town in driblets, when no demand exists, and sell for two-thirds of market rates. Such people are the only croakers we have; nor could such people with the same shiftless habits exist at all, as they do here somehow, in any other region under the sun.

Pickled Pears

10 pounds pears
3 pounds brown sugar
1 quart vinegar
1 ounce cinnamon
1 ounce ground cloves
1/4 pound candied citron, chopped

Editor's note:

If the pears are small you may prefer to pickle them whole.

Select pears that are ripe, but still very firm. Peel the pears, cut them in half and remove the core. Put them in a pan of water with lemon juice or a fruit preservative to keep them from turning brown. In a large stockpot, combine the sugar, vinegar and spices. Bring to a boil, stirring until the sugar is dissolved. Gently put in a few pears at a time. Simmer until the pears are tender. Place in sterilized jars. Cover to keep warm. When all the pears are cooked, add the citron to the syrup, bring it to a boil and pour over the pears in the jars. Seal and process in a boiling water bath.

JUNE 6, 1885

Strawberry Preserves

Editor's note:

This is the same way my mother-in-law taught me to make strawberry preserves. You will want to cut the berries in half or quarters so as to release more juice. Mix them well with the sugar and let them stand overnight in a cool place, but not in the refrigerator if you can avoid it. Simmer them gently in the syrup and they will keep a nice fresh flavor.

This is the only fruit I preserve the old fashioned way, as our mother's taught us — that is pound of fruit for pound of sugar. I put the sugar on the berries the night before they are to be cooked as it draws out the juice so nicely. In the morning, drain this off and put it on to scald in a porcelain kettle. When it boils and the scum is removed, I put in the berries and let them simmer until thoroughly cooked and the syrup becomes very rich. Then I put them into self-sealing bottles.

—Mrs. Johnson

Spiced Currants

5 pounds currants
4 pounds sugar
1 pint vinegar
2 ounces whole cloves
2 ounces stick cinnamon

Make a syrup of the sugar and vinegar. Tie the spices loosely in a bag and simmer them in the syrup for 10 minutes. Remove the spice bag and add the currants. Cook, over medium heat until the mixture is quite rich and thick. Put into sterilized jars and keep in the refrigerator.

Bed Bugs

There is living at my house a lady near 91 years old, who is as full of recipes as Elihu Burrit. For bed bugs, she says, "Take a ripe cucumber, press the juice out of it, then with a feather apply it to the bedstead in the bed bug range, and they will die instantly."

The above has had a fair trial enough in this vicinity to recommend it to a fair trial elsewhere.
—A.M., Walnut Grove, Ill.

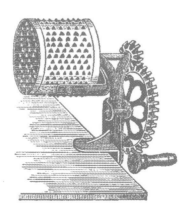

CHAPTER SIX

Meats

Recipes for whole meals and leftovers filled the pages of *Prairie Farmer*. Some of the earliest ones describe many ways to cook game. Later fancy dishes involving ways to prepare clams, lobster and salmon imported from the east or west coasts expand our understanding of rural and farm life at the end of the 19th century.

In many households, meat was served three meals a day. The centerpiece meal was dinner, frequently prepared at noon. Leftovers were served at supper with breakfast hash made out of the tag ends of meat, potatoes and other vegetables bound with an egg and formed into cakes fried in a bit of butter. Not much went to waste. Any remaining bits would be slopped to the hogs. However, in rural 19th century America, not all households were able to maintain that standard of living. During the 1880s, *Prairie Farmer* printed a number of articles on "getting by" in reduced circumstances. One of them detailed a week's menu for a family of five at 3 cents a head.

> *"Almost every family has a dinner of what is commonly called a 'boiled dish' and which, properly cooked, is one of the best dishes in the world."*
> *February 2, 1860*

As might be expected from a publication covering farm life, *Prairie Farmer* included in its pages numerous recipes for chicken. The surprising inclusion, to me, was the number of recipes for preparing steak. Beef cuts were likely not as tender as we are used to these days. One recipe called for beating the steak with a rolling pin for 10 minutes to tenderize it. Certainly the cut was as special then as it is now, and as likely to be mistreated.

In the column, The Martyrdom of the Steak, the author minces no words in advising cooks on the proper handling and preparation of meat. Although the slowly simmered beef a la mode was meant to be cooked at the back of the old wood-burning stove all morning, it makes a wonderful crock pot meal, filling the home with aromas now as then.

Important Truths in Connection with Agriculture

In the course of my readings I found the following condensed paragraph in "Chambers Information for the People" and for the sake of those for whom it was written, if you think it worth while, please publish it. —D.

1. Land to be well cultivated must either be the property of the farmer, or be let on a moderately long lease.

2. The husbandry must be convertible that is on a precise rotation of grain and green crops.

3. Cattle must be kept to produce a due share of manure for the fields.

4. If the land be moist or liable to heavy rains it must be effectually drained.

5. Deep plowing and thorough pulverizing of the soil are essential.

6. The fields must be properly fenced.

And lastly, no land will be profitable as a speculation unless closely superintended by a farmer whose mind is alive to all its varied wants, and neither rash in running into experiments not prejudiced against well authenticated improvements.

Hash

The number of housekeepers who cannot make a good mince pie and cannot cook a good hash is about equal. Now a poor dish of hash is a dish that can hardly be excelled in badness. It is about the last of all human fodder. That which is good will be selected by most eaters from a multitude of dishes.

To make a good hash
2 cups cold cooked corned beef
2 cups cold boiled potatoes
1/3 cup butter
1 cup hot milk
1/3 cup cooked turnips, optional
Salt and pepper

The beef and potatoes should be chopped fine. Melt the butter in a large frying pan, add the corned beef, potatoes, turnips if desired, and milk. Cook over medium heat, stirring occasionally to keep from sticking. Add more hot milk if necessary. The hash should be moist. Salt and pepper to taste.

Beefsteaks

Steaks should never be covered after they are laid upon the dish. A cover smothers them and thus they lose their best flavor. Beefsteaks should be eaten as soon as they are cooked.

The best pieces for steaks are the sirloin and rump. The top of the round next to the bone is very juicy and by pounding it with a mallet may be made as tender as the rump. These steaks should be cut nearly an inch thick. It is not necessary to grease the gridiron before putting on the steak — indeed the flavor of the meat is much injured by so doing.

Prepare a bed of coals. Put your gridiron over it, but do not let your gridiron get hot before you put on the steak. As soon as the meat becomes crisped a little, turn the steak. Do not burn the steak. Do not spill the gravy on the fire. Take up the steak on a hot dish turn the steak and replace it upon the gridiron. It will require 20 minutes to scald it through and brown the outside. When the steak is cooked, put it upon a hot dish and serve.

The Steak

Of Steak — of steak — of prime Rump Steak
A slice of half-inch thickness take
Without a blemish, soft and sound;
In weight a little more than a pound.
Who'd cook a Steak — Who'd cook a Steak
Must a fire clear proceed to make:
With red above and red below
In one delicious gentle glow.
If a coal should come a blaze to make,
Have patience! You musn't put on your Steak.

First rub — yes rub — with suet fat.
The gridiron's bars then on it flat
Impose the meat and the fire soon
Will make it sing a delicious tune.
And when 'tis brown'd by the genial glow,
Just turn the upper side below.
Both sides with brown being covered o'er,
For the moment, brown your Steak no more;

But on a hot dish let it rest.
And add of but a slice of the best;
In a minute or two the pepper box take,
And with it gently dredge your Steak.

When seasoned quite upon the fire
Some further time it will require;
And over and over be sure to turn
Your Steak till done — not let it burn;
For nothing drives me half so wild
As a nice Rump Steak in the cooking "spiled."
On fish or fowl and mutton and beef,
With plenty of cash and power to range,
But my Steak I never wished to change:
For a Steak was always a treat to me,
At breakfast luncheon, dinner, or tea.

Cooking Rabbits

Boiled Rabbit with onion sauce

They must be skewered and trussed so as to come to table in a crouching position. Dust it with flour as you would a boiled chicken to make it come out whiter. Tie it in a cloth if young, put it into boiling water; if old into cold water. The time of boiling must be entirely regulated by the apparent age and tenderness of the rabbit. Tomato instead of onion sauce is a much approved variation of this dish.

While the rabbit is boiling, prepare your onion sauce thus: Peel your onions, halve them and quarter them, put them on in a saucepan in cold water. Boil till perfectly soft, strain them from the water and braid them through a colander. To the pulp thus made, add a lump of butter and some thick cream with a little pepper and salt. Then make it just boil up, being careful it does not burn, and pour it over the rabbit as it lies on the dish. Serve, at the same time, a piece of boiled white bacon to eat with it and a tureen of melted butter.

Roast Rabbit

Make a force-meat of bread crumbs, minced beef suet, lemon peel, nutmeg, pepper and salt and a little lemon-thyme if sweet herbs are approved. Beat up two eggs, and mix with them the whole into a paste. Put this force-meat inside the rabbit and sew it up and skewer it into proper form. Rub the outside of the rabbit over with butter. Flour it a little, and stick on very thin slices of bacon by means of small skewers of iron wire.

A French cook would lard them with a larding needle. Those slices of bacon will roast up 'til they become quite crisp and dry, the fat which oozes from them will keep the rabbit moist and juicy. Still, it ought to be well basted while roasting. Make a gravy with a small piece of beef, a whole onion, put in without peeling, some whole pepper-corns, a blade of mace, and a clove or two, with a small crust of bread toasted very dry and brown, but not burnt. When the gravy is boiled enough, strain it, and make a little catsup and flour well braided together. Make the gravy just boil up before serving it with the roast rabbit in a separate tureen buy itself. Some add a glass of port wine to the gravy.

Stewed Rabbit

Cut the rabbit into joints. Half fry them into butter and lay them into a stew pan. Fry some sliced onions and put them over the rabbit in the stew pan with a little powdered mace; pepper and salt. Pour sufficient water over them to cover them, allowing for the waste by evaporation during cooking. The stew must be done very slowly, only being allowed to just simmer. It will take two hours to do it properly. When enough, take out each piece of rabbit and lay it on the dish on which it is to be served. With the gravy which remains in the stew pan mix a pickled walnut, finely and smoothly braided, with a good tablespoon of catsup and a dust of flour. Set it over the fire and pour it over your rabbit directly that it shows symptoms of boiling up.

Rabbit Pie

Cut the rabbits into joints and simply stew with water, pepper, salt and pounded mace till they are half done. Proceed then as for pigeon pie putting veal or pork or both instead of the beef. Cover with paste and bake till enough.

To Curry Rabbits

Take a young rabbit or two, skin and cut them into conveniently sized pieces to serve. Put them into a frying pan with some butter and fry them a nice brown color; then place them at the bottom of your stew pan. Slice and fry six or eight large onions; place them over the rabbit in the stew pan. Then mix four tablespoons of the best curry powder and some good stock gravy (which is a great point in securing success) with salt, cayenne pepper, nutmeg, three or four slices of lemon with the peel on, a small quantity of chopped pickles and a glass of sherry. Boil well and pour it over the rabbit and onions in the stew pan; let it all simmer together for three hours.

Serve it up in a dish encircled with rice that has been boiled in the following manner: Put the rice in cold water and when it boils, let it boil exactly sixteen minutes afterwards. The seventeenth minute would spoil it utterly. It is as with the charmed bullets of Zamail. "The six(teenth) shall achieve, the seven(teenth) shall deceive."

JULY 26, 1860

Pretty way of serving chicken

2 chickens, cut into serving pieces, or any other selection of chicken parts you prefer
2 slices bacon, diced
2 tablespoons butter
Water
1 teaspoon mace
Salt (optional)

Put the bacon in a large, deep frying pan with a cover. You will want a pan large enough to hold all your chicken in one layer. Fry the bacon very slowly to render out the fat. When the bacon is crisp, add the butter and begin browning the chicken a few pieces at a time. When each piece is browned on all sides, remove it to a platter and reserve. When all the pieces are browned, return them to the pan, add enough hot water to come halfway up the largest piece, add the mace and salt if desired. Cover the pan and simmer until the chicken is tender, about 1/2 hour, depending upon the size of the pieces. When the chicken is done, remove the pieces to a heated platter. Reduce the pan liquid to 2 cups and thicken by stirring in 2 tablespoons of butter blended with 2 tablespoons flour. Pour the gravy over the chicken and serve.

To Boil a Ham

Editor's note:

The original recipe suggests, "a handful of timothy hay improves it very much." I left that part out.

One 3- to 5-pound smoked ham with the rind scored to allow the flavors to permeate the meat. Cover the ham with cold water. Add 2 bay leaves, 2 sliced carrots, 1 large or 2 medium onions, 4 whole cloves, 4 cloves garlic, small bunch parsley, small bunch fresh thyme (or 1 teaspoon ground), 2 stalks celery (chopped), half a bottle of white wine. Bring to a boil, reduce heat and simmer 3 to 5 hours until the ham the very tender.

SEPTEMBER 27, 1860

Beef Stew

A very economical and most savory dish and delicious dish can be made with 2 or 3 pounds of chuck steak (a cheap part of beef) which infinitely surpasses the tasteless, insipid, common eating-house stuff called "beef a la mode." The dish is of Italian origin, and in that country is eaten with plain boiled macaroni and Parmesan cheese, or with a salad and with either it is "dainty dish to set before a king."

2 or 3 pounds chuck steak,
cut in 2-inch strips
1 1/2 teaspoons black pepper
1 teaspoon dried marjoram
1 teaspoon dried savory
1 teaspoon dried thyme
2 cups cold water

Editor's note:

The original recipe calls for using fresh herbs. Tie branches of the herbs together with white string and add to the simmering stew. You will want a bunch about 2 inches long and 3 inches wide, loosely packed.

Combine the beef, herbs and pepper with the water in a heavy stew pan. Bring to a boil, lower heat and simmer until the meat is tender, about 2 hours. You will need to watch this and stir it from time to time, maybe even adding some additional water to keep it from burning.

Preserving Meats

A method of preserving meats discovered by Mr. Alppert and patented in England is as follows:

The meat to be preserved is first parboiled or somewhat more and freed from the bones. It is then put, together with vegetables, if required, into tin cases or canisters, which are filled quite up with rich gravy.

A tin cover with a small aperture is carefully fitted on by solder and while the vessel is perfectly full it is placed in boiling water and undergoes the remainder of the cooking. The small hole in the cover is completely closed up while the whole is yet hot. The canister with its ingredients is now allowed to cool, in consequence of which these contract, and the sides are the vessel are slightly forced inward by the pressure of the atmosphere, and become a little concave. The vessel being thus hermetically sealed, and all access of air prevented, it may be sent into any climate without fear of putrefaction in a distant region, many months, or even years after its preparation.

In this manner may all kinds of alimentary substances be preserved: beef, mutton, veal and poultry, fish and game, soups, broths, vegetables, creams and custards. Of a quantity taken by Captain Nash to India, not one canister was spoiled, and one which he brought back contained, after two years, beef in the highest state of perfection and preservation, after being carried upward of 35,000 miles in the warmest climates.

FEBRUARY 18, 1871

Stuffed Beefsteak

3- to 4-pound rump roast slice
For the stuffing:
4 pieces of stale, good quality (firmly textured) bread
1/2 teaspoon salt
1/2 teaspoon pepper
1 tablespoon marjoram
1/4 cup melted butter

To make the stuffing, tear the bread into small pieces no larger than a half inch. Mix with the dry spices and pour the melted butter over. Set aside to cool. Prepare the meat by making a pocket for the stuffing. Take a sharp knife and cut into the piece of beef along one of the longer sides to within 1 inch of the three remaining sides. Fill with the stuffing and close with skewers. Place the meat into a large pan or crockpot; barely cover with water, wine or tomato juice. Simmer until tender.

To Sweeten Meat and Fish

Meat, fish, etc., from intense heat or long keeping, are likely to pass into a state of corruption. A simple and sure mode of keeping them sound and healthy is by putting few pieces of charcoal, each the size of an egg, into the pot or saucepan wherein the fish or flesh is to be boiled. Among others, an experiment of this kind was tried upon a turbot, which appeared too far gone to be eatable. The cook, as advised, put three or four pieces of charcoal, each the size of an egg, under the strainer, in the fish kettle. After boiling the proper time, the turbot came to the table perfectly sweet and firm.

OCTOBER 20, 1877

Clara Francis' Curry Powder

1/2 ounce cinnamon
1/2 ounce allspice
1/2 ounce cardamon
3 ounces coriander
2 ounces turmeric
1 ounce black pepper
1 ounce dry mustard
1 ounce ginger

Combine all the powders. Mix thoroughly. Store in a tightly sealed jar in a cool, dark place.

Curried Chicken

1 chicken, cut into pieces
2 slices of bacon
1 to 2 cups water

For the gravy:
2 tablespoons butter
1 cup milk
3 tablespoons flour
1 tablespoon curry powder

Serve with boiled rice garnished with parsley.

Wash the chicken and set aside. Brown the bacon over low heat in a frying pan with a lid. Use a pan large enough to hold the chicken in one layer. When the bacon is cooked, add the chicken and add just enough water to cover the pieces. Bring to a boil; lower the heat to just simmer. Cover the frying pan and simmer the chicken until tender, about 30 to 45 minutes. When the chicken is done, remove it to a serving platter and make the curry sauce.

Add the butter to the accumulated juices in the pan. Combine the flour and curry powder with the milk and mix well to remove all lumps. Pour into the frying pan and cook over medium heat, stirring constantly until the sauce is thickened. Pour the sauce over the chicken.

DECEMBER 13, 1860

Broiled Steak

February 21, 1885
A milkman is going round with his broken jaw tied up. There is great curiosity among his customers to know whether it was done by a cow's foot or a pump-handle.

Broiled steak should be cut from a well-kept rump and they are generally liked about 3/4 inch thick. Most cooks beat them with a rolling pin for 10 minutes, but if the meat is of good quality and the rump has been well kept, there will be no necessity for this. Just before finishing, rub a lump of butter over and lightly dredge with pepper and salt. Pickles and scraped horseradish make a good garnish. And for sauce, suit your taste.

Martyrdom at the Steak

Here are a few practical suggestions on how the ordeal may be avoided.

The cook who fails to serve a choice steak, chop or other superior cut of meat in any but a proper manner, is totally unworthy of the name. Those persons who live where they can command the best — and afford to pay for it — have but slight occasion to understand the modus operandi by which indifferent meats can be rendered palatable and nourishing.

There are many, however, who are compelled by necessity — motives of economy or limitations of supplies — to content themselves with inferior portions. To such we would recommend the study of the art of seasoning, and of the various methods by which tough meats may be rendered tender, savory, nourishing and altogether delicious.

The average American cook will sprinkle meat plentifully with salt and pepper before cooking and consider that anything further by way of seasoning is nonsense. If she be told never to salt meat previous to cooking, will still hold definitely to the opinion that the seasoning must be cooked in.

This is in itself enough to injure the best of meat, and will make a lower grade totally unpalatable ad indigestible. The action of the salt during the process of cooking, renders the fibre tough and tasteless; therefore salt should never be added until the meat is almost or completely done.

While this rule should be observed in regard to salt, it should also be understood that pepper and other spices require the action of heat to bring out their true flavor. The degree should not be so great however, as to cause the evaporation of the aroma, thereby injuring their essential qualities.

A piece of tough meat that by unskillful treatment would be completely ruined and rendered unfit for use can, by long and slow cooking be converted, with the help of a savory herb or two and a little spice, into a dish in which the flavors are so nicely intermingled and the meat so tender as to be perfectly appetizing and wholesome.

Comparatively speaking, Americans bestow but slight attention to the art of seasoning, confining their experiments to a liberal use of salt and pepper and altogether ignoring that delicate blending of flavors in which foreign artists excel; hence the preference given in this country to French cooks.

To be sure, there are those among the latter class who carry their ideas to extremes and so effectively disguise everything that one is never quite sure what one is eating. An excess of seasoning is just as objectionable in the cooking of meats as a superabundance of spice in puddings or pies.

Every housekeeper should have in her storeroom a good supply of aromatic herbs: summer savory, sage, thyme, mint, sweet basil and bay leaves. In the garden in summer, in a box in the kitchen window in winter, there should always be growing curled parsley.

With the temperate use of these seasonings, many dishes can be improved that without them would be insipid. Bay leaves can be obtained from the druggist. The herbs should be grown in one's own garden; dried, powdered and sifted under personal supervision and put away in corked bottles so as to preserve their strength.

—Clara Francis

How to Preserve Women

Advice from the Home Journal:

There is nothing in the world that we think so much of as women. Our mother is a woman — wife, sister and daughter. A fine magnificent specimen of the sex, full of life and health; ripe red cheek and flashing eyes is something that does one good to look at as she illuminates the humdrum sidewalks and everyday streets. There is no rubbing it out; women are the ornament, charm, blessing, beauty, and bliss of life (men's life we mean, of course). Any means, therefore that can be derived for preserving them should be publicly known.

They are different from any other kind of fruit. You cannot pickle them. You cannot do them up in sugar and set them in a cold room with a paper of brandy over their mouths. You cannot put them in a can sealed up air-tight without injuring their form and flavor. Now, as men are so dependent upon women for their choicest blessings, a proper mode of preserving them becomes of great moment and we are sure the public will thank us for an infallible recipe.

Let her visit neighbors, go shopping, call upon the poor, and walk for the good of it, the fun of it.

Keep away from the stove or register. Air that is dry or burnt, more or less charged with gasses evolved by fuel is poison. Go upstairs and make the beds with mittens on. Fly around the house like mad and ventilate the rooms. Don't sit pent up in a single room with double windows. Fruit will not retain its form or flavor in air-tight cans, neither will women. They need air.

Again, do not live in dark rooms. Light fades the carpet, but it feeds the flowers. No living animal or vegetable can enjoy health in darkness. Light is as necessary as air, and a brown tan is preferable even as a matter of beauty to a sickly paleness of complexion.

Every woman should be married to an excellent man. Marriage, it is true, brings care and wear, but it is the ring that is worn that remains bright, and the watch that lies still unwound that gets out of order. The sweet sympathies involved in the family relation the new energies developed by new responsibilities the new compassion for all outlays of strength, bring about a delightful play upon the heart and intellect, which in their reaction upon the body produces an effect that is nothing less than preservation. There is a higher moral power than this. No one is completely armed against the encroaching ills of life who has in the heart no place for religion.

There you have the recipe. It has within it the cure for many a disease — the prevention of many more.

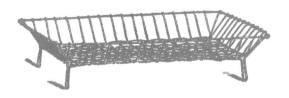

Stewed Steak with Oysters

2 pounds rump steak
1 pint oysters
1 tablespoon lemon juice
3 tablespoons butter
1 tablespoon flour
Salt and pepper to taste
1 cup water

Wash the oysters in the water and strain into the stew pan. Put this liquor on to heat. As soon as it comes to a boil, skim and set back. Put the butter in a flying pan and when hot, put in the steak. Cook 10 minutes. Take up the steak and stir the flour into the butter remaining in the pan. Stir until a dark brown. Add the oyster liquor and boil one minute. Season with salt and pepper. Put back the steak, cover the pan and simmer a 1/2 hour, then add the oysters and lemon juice. Boil 1 minute. Serve on a hot dish with points of toast for a garnish.

AUGUST 26, 1883

Pressed Beef

Boil beef of any good kind till the bones fall out. Pick it over carefully, removing all gristle. Chop it fine, season with salt and such herbs as taste suggests. Press it in a pan with a heavy weight. When cold, cut in slices and serve.

JULY 1854

From the Prairie Farmer *household column:*

There is room for the exercise of Woman's Rights in a direction which is certainly overlooked. We mean in perfecting the art of cookery. Our American cookery is much often wretched. Women learn to cook one or two kinds of meat, make a loaf of bread, a pie and six sorts of cake and preserves and think the science of cookery exhausted. If any improvement is mentioned, the probability is that it refers to some sort of new cake.

Why cannot we have more good common dishes say of soups, meats and especially of vegetables: Will the Rights women indulge their genius in that direction?

Recipes for Chicken Pie

 *Editor's note:*

Several recipes for chicken pie appeared in *Prairie Farmer* over the
years. They really are more like a chicken and dumpling dinner, as
the emphasis on the amount of gravy indicates. The crust is more
like a biscuit than piecrust. I was puzzled that the chicken was left
in whole pieces not boned shreds. But if you think about this as a
dinner, it makes sense. Why should the busy farm wife have to
precook and bone all that meat, when those who are doing the
eating could just as well do the job themselves?

APRIL 14, 1877

Chicken Pie

2 pieces of bacon or salt pork
1 chicken cut into serving pieces
Water

For the gravy:
Salt and pepper
1 cup milk
1 tablespoon cornstarch
1 tablespoon butter

In a large frying pan with deep sides, sauté
the bacon until it is crisp. Add the dry
chicken pieces carefully and brown on all
sides. Pour over enough hot water to come
one-fourth of the way up the chicken pieces.
Cover the pan and cook over medium heat
until the chicken is tender. Remove the
chicken and set aside. (At this point you can
remove the bones, although the original
recipe suggests the bones are left in.) Combine the cornstarch with the milk and stir it
into the remaining liquid in the frying pan.
Add the butter and salt and pepper to taste.
Put the chicken in a deep pie plate or casserole dish. Pour the gravy around. Cover with
a top crust only. Preheat the oven to 425
degrees F. Bake for 30 minutes or until the
pie juices bubble and the crust is browned.

Raised crust for chicken pie
1 cup milk
1 tablespoon butter
1 teaspoon baking powder
2 1/2 cups flour

Melt the butter and stir into the milk.
Combine the flour and baking powder. Stir
in the milk to form a stiff dough. Knead a
little and roll out 1/2 inch thick.

Smothered Chicken

Large whole chicken
1/2 cup water

2 tablespoons butter
1 cup boiling water additional
1 tablespoon cornstarch

Editor's note:

It is the method
of cooking here that makes
all the difference.

Preheat the oven to 375 degrees F. Split the chicken down the back and open up flat. Lay in a large baking dish, breast side down. Put the 1/2 cup of water and butter in the pan. Put a second heavy baking dish directly on top of the chicken and fill it with water to weigh it down. Bake the chicken for three-fourths of the time needed (at 20 minutes per pound), checking from time to time to see if you need to add more water. Remove the weighted pan. Carefully turn the chicken over and finish baking, basting frequently with the accumulated juices until tender.

Remove the chicken to a heated platter. Add the boiling water to the cooking pan and stir to remove any crusty bits. Add the cornstarch dissolved in a little water, pepper and salt. Put in a small saucepan and cook over medium heat until the gravy is thick. Pour on to chicken and serve.

May 22, 1877
Chicken Pie
Pour the gravy over the
chicken, be sure to have
plenty of gravy and cover
the pie with a crust, cutting
it well on top. Glaze with
the beaten white and a
little of the yolk, or part
of an egg beaten with a
little milk.

Beef Loaf

August 25, 1883
When a lady living in Chelsea sent to London for a doctor, she apologized for asking him to come such a distance. "Don't speak of it," answered the M.D. "I happen to have another patient in the neighborhood, and can thus kill two birds with one stone."

3 pounds very lean hamburger
1/4 pound ground salt pork or bacon
(you may substitute regular ground pork)
1 cup fine cracker crumbs
3 eggs, well beaten
Salt and pepper to taste
1/2 teaspoon ground sage

Preheat oven to 325 degrees F. Mix all ingredients quickly; do not over mix or the meat will become tough. Pack into a well-greased loaf pan. Sprinkle additional cracker crumbs on top. Bake 2 1/2 hours, basting from time to time with a tablespoon of butter dissolved in 3/4 cup hot water.

MARCH 17, 1877

Cause of Lamp Explosions

There are many causes for the explosions of kerosene lamps, and a knowledge of them may in some instances prevent accidents. It is not the oil that explodes, but the vapor or gas that is generated from the oil. The vapor, when confined or under pressure, is as explosive and dangerous as gunpowder.

The ignition of this gas may occur as follows:
1. A lamp may be standing on a table or mantle, and a slight puff of air from the open window or door may cause an explosion.

2. A lamp may be taken up quickly from a table or mantel and instantly exploded.
3. A lamp is taken out into the entry where there is a draft or out of doors and an explosion ensues.
4. A lighted lamp is taken up a flight of stairs or is raised quickly to place it on the mantel resulting in an explosion.
In these cases the mischief is done by the air movement — either by suddenly checking the draft or by forcing air down the chimney against the flame.

Lobster Salad

2 cups water
2 cups rich milk
1 teaspoon salt (optional)
1/2 teaspoon white pepper
1/4 butter
Meat of freshly boiled lobster
picked in flakes (about 1 1/2 cups)
2 tablespoons fresh parsley
1 1/2 cups cracker crumbs

Editor's Note:

This is not a typical salad, although it is an excellent way of stretching one lobster to feed several people.

Combine all the ingredients except the cracker crumbs in a medium saucepan. Simmer for 5 minutes so that the lobster flavors the liquid. Stir in the cracker crumbs. Pour the mixture into a lightly greased casserole dish and put under the broiler until the top is just browned.

Lamb Chops with Peas

Shell the freshest of green peas, being careful to keep them free from dust so they will not require washing, as this will destroy their sweetness. Drop them into boiling water, a little more than enough to cover them, add very little salt and white sugar and over the top put some fresh green pods, first washing them. Cover close and boil for twenty minutes.

Remove the pods. If there was not too much water, put on the peas in the first place and if they are not too old, they will be bright and tender. Add a good piece of butter and salt and pepper to taste.

While the peas are cooking, trim some nice rib chops so that they will be of uniform shape. Remove all skin and scrape the lower part of the bone clean for two or three inches of its length. Broil over a bright fire. Take from the gridiron. Pepper, salt and butter the chops and lay them in regular order (overlapping each other) on a hot platter. Place the peas around them and serve very hot. To add to the appearance of the dish, wrap a piece of fringed white paper around the bone of each chop.

FIG. 29.—PERSPECTIVE VIEW OF ELEVATION.

FIG. 30. GROUND PLAN—FIRST FLOOR.

EXPLANATION.
DIMENSIONS IN THE CLEAR.

A, Dinning Room, 14 x 17 feet.
B, Bed Room, 8 x 11 feet.
C, Hall, 6 x 8 feet.
D, Parlor, 15 x 17 feet.
E, Bed Room, 10 x 16 feet.
F F, Passages, 3½ feet wide.
G, Kitchen, 16 x 17 feet.
H, Front Stairs, 3 feet clear.
I, Closet under Stairs.
J, Bed Room Closet.
K, L, Cheese Room and Pantry.
M, Wood House, 24 x — feet.
N, O, Fireplace and Oven.
P, P, Piazza, 7 feet wide.
Q, Piazza, 6 feet wide.
R, Back and Cellar Stairs.
S, Wood House Stairs.
T, Closet.
V, Cistern.
W, Outside Cellar Door.
X X, Cupboards.
1, Place for Stove.
2, False Fireplace.

Drawn on a scale of fifteen feet to the inch.

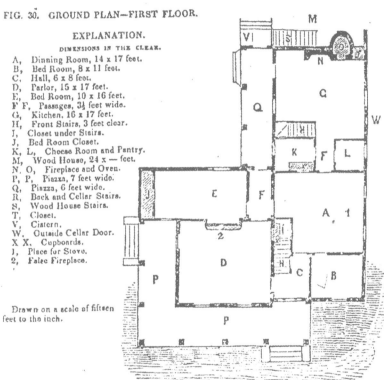

FIG. 31.—GROUND PLAN—SECOND FLOOR.

EXPLANATION.
A, Room 11 x 11 ft.
B, do 11 x 14 ft.
C, do 14 x 17 ft.
D, do 10 x 14 ft.
I I I, Closets.
F F F, Passages.
G, Garret over Kitchen.
1 1, Stove Pipes and Chimneys.
S, Stairs.

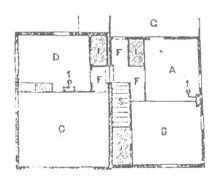

A Prairie Kitchen

Sir Garnet Woolsy's Irish Stew

*In the "Soldier's Pocket Book" by Sir Garnet Wolseley,
the following recipe is given for Irish stew.*

16 1/2 pounds meat
16 1/2 pounds potatoes
4 pounds onions
8 ounces salt
1 ounce pepper
1/2 pound flour

Cut away the meat from the bone and then into pieces of 1/4 pound each, the loin and neck of the mutton into chops, disjoint the shoulder, and cut the blade bone into four pieces (if leg, into slices) 1/4 inch thick. Rub them with salt, pepper and flour and place the meat in the boiler with some fat; brown it on both sides. Then add the onions whole and then the potatoes and enough water to cover the potatoes. Stew gently for two hours, keep the fire down, and the pot well covered during the cooking.

JULY 14, 1883

Chicken Salad

4 cups cooked chicken
2 cups celery, chopped
4 cups cabbage, finely chopped

For the dressing:
4 hard-boiled eggs, separated
1/2 cup oil
1 tablespoon black pepper
2 teaspoons prepared mustard
1 cup vinegar
1/4 cup prepared horseradish, or less
(not cream-style)
Yield: 10 1-cup servings

Combine the chicken and vegetables and set aside in the refrigerator to chill. Mash the egg yolks and combine with the oil, pepper, and mustard. Gradually stir in the vinegar. (You may use the blender or food processor to do this.) Add the horseradish to taste. Just before serving, drain any accumulated juices from the chicken and vegetables and stir in the dressing. Garnish with strips of hard-boiled egg white.

Broiled Spring Chicken

This is such a familiar dish to the majority of housekeepers, it may be considered almost superfluous for me to give my mode of preparing it, but it is so good and juicy that we think it better than the usual method.

First, after cutting the chicken up for convenience of serving, loosen or partly cut all the joints, making them as flat as possible by pounding. Wipe very dry and broil the whole carefully to a light brown, avoiding scorching any part. When thoroughly done, take it up in a square tin or dripping pan, butter it well, season with pepper and salt and set it in the oven for a few minutes.

Lay slices of moistened buttered bread on a platter. Take the chicken up over it, add to the gravy in the pan part of a cup of cream if you have it, if not use milk. Thicken with a little flour and pour over the chicken. We all pronounce this excellent.

—Mrs. Neal

Iowa Housekeeper's Notes Those Three-Cent Meals

By Mrs. Emma King, King's Ranch, Pottawattamie County

A former paper (January 3) calls for someone to tell how a family of five can have meals for 3 cents per head, or 15 cents for the whole family. I believe I can solve the problem, but do not think that very many of the Prairie Farmer family who are in good health would desire to give up the many little luxuries of the table, which are both wholesome and very palatable and can be had for very little outlay of money.

Fruits especially seem very desirable, though only the cheapest kinds could be used at this price. I will append below a bill of fare for five days which, if one only desires plenty of food to sustain life, and that nutritious in quality, I think they would find all sufficient. It certainly is true that the American people as a class, live on too rich and indigestible food. Of course a family residing in the country where they have enough ground for a garden, say1 acre, can live quite nicely on 3 cents per meal if they only count what real outlay of cash is needed.

After the seeds are once purchased, there need be no further expense, and even a day laborer can get a little time after work hours in spring and summer and the wife and children (if any) can sow the seed and weed and cultivate the plants themselves. The green peas, beans, radishes, tomatoes, potatoes, beets, etc. that can be raised are themselves "as good as gold" at least towards making a good living. With these and the addition of a few things from the country store, a comfortable supply for the table may be had.

If the family possesses a good cow, they need buy nothing but flour and meal with a little sugar and salt. But we are supposing that those for whom our bill of fare is made can sing with the old itinerant: No foot of land do I possess, no cottage in the wilderness, a poor wayfaring man.

Editor's note:

This set of menus is interesting for a perspective on home economics of the era. While certainly there were those in affluent households, many still struggled to make a living. These menus are throwbacks to the meals described in many of the early Midwestern pioneers' diaries. We need not think of this austere variety as a hardship, however. For although plain to our tastes, they were relished in the period. In fact, one Quaker teacher in Des Moines in the 1870s writes of being thankful for food in this style.

MONDAY

Breakfast
Graham mush made with 1 quart of graham flour stirred smoothly in boiling water and cooked 1/2 hour, 4 1/2 cents; 1 quart milk, 5 cents; 1 loaf white bread, 5 cents. Total 14 1/2 cents.

Dinner
Soup made of shank of beef, 10 cents; 1/5 pint rice, 2 cents; 5 pounds potatoes boiled or baked, 3 cents; Total 15 cents.

Supper
Corn meal mush made from 3 quarts meal stirred into water and cooked 2 1/2 to 3 hours,3 cents; 2 quarts milk, 10 cents; salt, 1 cent. Total 15 cents.

TUESDAY

Breakfast
Corn meal batter cakes from 3 pints meal, 2 1/2 cents; 1 pint wheat flour, 3 cents; 3 pints sour milk 3 1/2 cents; soda and salt, 1/4 cents; milk gravy 1 quart milk, 5 cents; flour for thickening and salt 3/4 cent. Total 15 cents.

Dinner
Loaf wheat bread, 5 cents; 1 quart beans, boiled, 3 3/4 cents; salt and milk for seasoning and milk for gravy to eat on bread, 6 1/4 cents. Total 15 cents.

Supper
Unleavened graham gems made from water and 3 pints graham flour, 6 cents; common dried applesauce, enough to relish with the gems; 9 cents. Total 15 cents.

WEDNESDAY

Breakfast
Mush made for "Avena" a delicious preparation of oats; 1 pound of which will make a very large quantity, 7 1/7 cents; 1 quart milk, 5 cents; sugar, 7 cents. Total 15 cents.

Dinner
6 pounds potatoes, 4 cents; unleavened graham gems as above, 6 cents; 1/2 pound or teacup of rice, 5 cents. Total 14 1/2 cents.

Supper
3 pounds hominy, which has been cooked 6 to 8 hours, 9 cents; 1 quart milk, 5 cents; salt, 1/2 cent. Total 14 1/2 cents.

THURSDAY

Breakfast
Corn meal for fried mush, 3 cents; meat fryings to fry in, 2 cents; 5 pounds potatoes, 3 1/2 cents; milk gravy 6 cents; salt, 3/4 cents. Total 15 cents.

Dinner
1 1/2 pounds boiling meat at 8 cents per pound, 12 cents. After boiling very tender and removing the bones to the soup left add some potatoes sliced and cooked until done, 2 cents. Thicken with a little flour, 1 cent. Total 15 cents.

Supper
1 loaf white bread, 5 cents; 1/2 pound boiled rice, 5 cents; 1 quart milk, 5 cents. Total 15 cents.

FRIDAY

Breakfast
Graham and corn meal porridge made by boiling 1 quart milk, 5 cents; 1 pint milk thickened with about 1/2 pint graham flour, 2 cents; the same of corn meal, 1/2 cent; or just enough to make a thick porridge and letting it boil 10 to 15 minutes adding a little salt, 1/4 cent; 5 pounds potatoes, boiled the previous day, sliced and warmed up with a little of the quart of milk from the gruel, 3 cents; part of a loaf of white bread, 4 1/2 cents. Total 15 cents.

Dinner
Cornbread made with 1 quart meal, 1 1/2 cents; 1/2 pint wheat flour, 1/2 cents; 2 teaspoons baking powder, 2 cents; 1 tablespoonful shortening, 1 cent. Mix with cold water to a thin batter and bake in hot oven. 1 quart beans, 3 3/4 cents; cornstarch blancmange made with 1 pint milk, 2 1/2 cents; 1 pint water and 4 tablespoons cornstarch, 2 cents; sugar for encrusting, 1 3/4 cents. Total 15 cents.

Supper
White gems made with 1 quart flour, 4 1/4 cents; 1 pint milk, 2 1/2 cents; 1 pint water or enough to make a thicker batter than for griddle cakes, a trifle of salt, bake in iron gem pans in a hot oven; 1 pound dried peaches, stewed, 8 cents. Total 15 cents.

Pork and Parsnip Stew

2 cups peeled and sliced parsnips
2 cups peeled and diced potatoes
1 pound pork steak or chop,
cut into 1-inch cubes
4 cups water

3 tablespoons butter
3 tablespoons flour
1 1/2 cups milk
1/2 teaspoon pepper
Salt to taste

Combine the parsnips, potatoes and pork with the water. Bring to a boil, lower the heat and simmer until the vegetables are done and the meat is tender. Drain the water, reserving 1/2 cup. In a medium saucepan melt the butter and add the flour, stirring until the mixture bubbles. Gradually add the milk and reserved cooking water. Continue cooking until the sauce is thickened. Add the vegetables and pork to the sauce. Season with pepper and salt.

Chicken Croquettes

As winter is our visiting season, I want to suggest a nice tea dish that I have just learned how to prepare. —Mrs. Mallory

3 cups minced chicken
1/4 cup chicken broth
1/4 cup cream
1/4 cup flour
Salt and pepper to taste
Cracker crumbs
2 well-beaten eggs
Cooking spray or hot lard

Combine the chicken, broth, cream, flour, salt and pepper in a medium saucepan. Cook over medium heat until thickened, stirring to keep from burning. Allow to cool. Using your hands, form into small cone shapes about 2 inch high. Roll these in cracker crumbs, then into the eggs and back into the cracker crumbs. Allow to stand 10 minutes or so for the coating to firm. The original recipe says to deep-fry in hot lard. However, you can bake them successfully. Preheat the oven to 425 degrees F. Place the croquettes on a foil-lined baking sheet. Spray with cooking spray and bake until the coating is crispy. They are best served as soon as done.

Salmon Dish for Tea

Salmon is one of the cheapest foods we have. It comes out of the can almost as fresh and good as if just taken from the water, and better than when carried far to market and kept exposed for sale. There is another decided advantage, you can keep it on hand any length of time, and it is always ready to use in an emergency.

—Mrs. Gage

I am glad this subject is brought up, for many housekeepers have not yet learned the value, economy and convenience of canned salmon. For six years past we have bought it by the dozen cans when it costs only 15 to 18 cents a can. I always buy the "last crop" and get the best, as a cent or two on a can is more than made up in the better quality and the less of refuse. The second and third grades contain more bone and skin and are less desirable. I make a dish that is also very desirable for luncheon or tea.

—Mrs. Strong

1 can salmon
1 tablespoon vinegar
1/2 cup mayonnaise
1 tablespoon mustard
1/8 teaspoon cayenne pepper

Drain the salmon and pick it over to remove any bones and skin. Mix it with the vinegar and form into a nice loaf shape on some curly lettuce leaves. Combine the mayonnaise, mustard and cayenne. Spread over the top and sides of the salmon loaf. Garnish with finely chopped hard-boiled egg and grated horseradish.

Roast Beef with Lemon

For an occasional change from the ordinary mode of cooking roast beef, the following is recommended. To a roast of 5 or 6 pounds, squeeze over it the juice of a large lemon. Grate the outside off then roll the remainder of the lemon up in the roast. It will give a pleasant flavor to the meat and neutralizes somewhat the oily taste of the gravy if the beef is at all fat.

—Mrs. Emmons

Mock Duck

Editor's note:

The inclusion of a "Mock Duck" recipe in an 1885 issue of *Prairie Farmer* underscores the changes that occurred in farm life and farm diet between the 1840s and 1880s. Most early settlers took advantage of the plentiful supply of game and fowl. You might note the 1855 *Prairie Farmer* column we've included with many recipes for preparing rabbit. By the time of this recipe, however, farm life had become more "settled." Farmers were raising chickens, hogs and even beef. So a cook might prefer to make "mock duck" rather than send a husband or son out to get a real one.

3 1/2 pounds good rump steak, sliced thick
2 cups fine fresh bread crumbs
1/4 cup minced onion
3 tablespoons butter
1/2 teaspoon pepper
1/2 teaspoon summer savory
1 egg yolk
1/4 cup milk

Make a stuffing from the bread crumbs, onion, butter, seasonings and egg yolk. Add as much of the milk as necessary to moisten it. Spread the stuffing over the slice of meat and roll it up, tucking in the ends to keep the stuffing inside. Tie the meat roll securely. Put in a crockpot and pour the stock over it. Cook slowly 2 to 3 hours. You may then baste it with butter and brown it in a 350-degree F oven for 20 minutes.

Fried Chicken

There are few better dishes than fried chicken, if cooked satisfactorally; but it needs careful watching, because, if either under or overdone, it is tasteless and unpalatable. Cut up the chicken into pieces for proper serving, wipe them dry, and season slightly. Have ready a spider or deep pan with two tablespoons of butter; make it hot; then lay in the chicken not too closely and cover so as to retain the steam.

Do not cook very fast, but let the heat be uniform and steady until is its nicely browned on this side then turn and add more pepper and salt if needed and more butter also. When done tie it up, pour a teacupful of milk or cream into the pan. When it boils up, add a little thickening take it up in a gravy tureen and serve it with the chicken. It adds materially to the flavor.
—Mrs. Raikes

Beef Pot Roast

1/2 teaspoon salt
2 teaspoons black pepper
3- to 4-pound sirloin tip roast,
or other roast
Water
10 whole cloves
10 whole peppercorns

Rub the meat with the salt and pepper. Heat a large Dutch oven or stock pot. Brown the meat slowly on all sides without using any fat or oil. Take your time with this step, turning the meat several times until it is well browned. The original directions call for taking 30 minutes. I suggest taking at least 15 to 20 minutes. Pour warm water around the meat, coming about halfway up. Add the cloves and peppercorns. Do not cover the meat. Lower the heat and simmer for 3 to 4 hours until the meat is tender, turning the meat a couple of times during the process. Let the meat stand 15 minutes before carving. Strain the cooking juices to remove the spices, thicken and serve as gravy.

Potted Chicken

In this hot weather, I avail myself of all the dishes possible that can be eaten cold, hence pressed beef, pressed chicken and potted chicken are all frequently made. For the latter, strip the meat from the bones of cold roast fowl to every pound of meat, allow 1/4 pound butter, salt and cayenne to taste, 1 teaspoon powdered mace, 1/2 small nutmeg. Cut the meat into small pieces, pound it well with the butter, sprinkle in the spices gradually and keep pounding until reduced to a smooth paste. Put it into a small jars and cover with clarified butter. Two or three slices of ham minced and pounded with the above will be an improvement. Keep in a dry place.
—Mrs. Mallory

 **Editor's note:**

This is really a form of paté.
The food processor will
make it much easier.

Roast Beef with Yorkshire Pudding

Use a rib roast for this dish. Place it in the dripping pan, sprinkle with salt and pepper and dredge with flour. Preheat the oven to 450 degrees F. Bake for 15 minutes, then lower the temperature to 350 degrees F and bake 15 minutes per pound for medium. About an hour before the meat is done make the Yorkshire Pudding.

Yorkshire Pudding
3 eggs
2 cups milk
3/4 cup flour
Dash pepper

Mix all the ingredients. Have the meat in a separate pan. Pour off the fat and juices from the dripping pan, keeping in about 3 tablespoons. Pour in the batter and bake at 425 degrees F for 40 to 50 minutes, until golden and puffed. Cut in rectangular pieces and serve alongside the beef.

Hamburg Steaks

When onions are not objectionable,
a very nice dish can be made by the following process. — Mrs. Everts

2 pounds chopped beef round steak
1 teaspoon onion juice or 1 tablespoon finely grated onion
1/4 teaspoon white pepper

Mix all ingredients and form into patties. Cook on the stove in a frying pan in 3 tablespoons melted butter. You can then make a gravy by adding 2 tablespoons flour to the pan drippings and then adding 1 cup hot water, stirring until thick. To cook on a grill, put a small piece of butter on top of each hamburg steak as you place it on the grill. The butter will melt into the meat and make a very tasty burger.

Beef A La Mode

4 slices bacon
2 onions, minced
1/4 teaspoon ground cloves
1/4 teaspoon ground allspice
1/2 teaspoon ground pepper
1/2 teaspoon ground savory
1/2 teaspoon ground thyme
1/2 teaspoon ground tarragon
3 pounds flank steak
2 carrots, sliced
1 turnip, diced
1 bunch celery, sliced
3 cups water
3/4 cup port wine

Dice the bacon slices and fry in a frying pan over low heat. When the pan is covered with bacon drippings, add the onion and continue cooking over medium heat until the bacon bits are crisp and the onion is transparent. Remove from heat and drain off fat. Blot with paper towels to eliminate as much fat as possible. Set aside to cool. Combine the spices and set aside. With a sharp knife, cut the surface of the flank steak making five or six cuts lengthwise across the piece of meat. Hold the knife at an angle so that the cut is more parallel than perpendicular to the surface of the meat. Do not cut completely through the piece of meat. Rub the spices and herb combination into the slits. Stuff the slits with onion and bacon. Roll the meat into a cylinder from the long edge, parallel to the cuts. Tie securely with kitchen string. Put the meat roll into a stewpot or slow cooker. Add the vegetables, water and wine.

Simmer very slowly for five hours, or until the meat is tender. When tender, transfer the meat and vegetables from the pot to a heated plate. Allow to stand for 10 minutes. Cut the meat across the grain in slices to so that the pinwheel of spices, onions and bacon shows. Remove all the fat from the broth and serve broth as a soup or as a sauce over the vegetables and meat.

The broth leftover from making this dish can be served as soup, or simply poured over the meat as a sauce. The secret to successfully preparing this dish is cutting wide, shallow slits into the uncooked beef so that it can be properly stuffed.

Nice Way to Use Cold Ham

I have seen this in the Question Box every week for a long time, and hoped someone would suggest a newer way than mine for utilizing the knuckle ends of boiled ham, but as no answer has come. I will give my methods. I sometimes trim all the meat off, picking out superfluous fat and gristle, then put it in the chopping bowl and mince it fine. To a teacup full of meat, add a tablespoon of melted butter and as much mixed mustard. Work the whole thoroughly together, and use it as a tea relish. Thus prepared, it will keep several days and is good for sandwiches also.

—Mrs. Lane

Things One May Eat with the Fingers

There are certain customs among well-bred people which it is well for all to know. Children on the farm where meals are often taken in a hurry, may just as well understand and constantly practice a portion of these at least. They will then feel less embarrassed when away from home. Old people whose habits have become strongly fixed may not readily fall into new ones though certain habits are easily acquired if one sets about it and even aged persons who sit at table with the young should make some effort to teach the latter by example.

We will not here speak particularly of the fact that it is considerably impolite to convey any kind of food to the mouth with a knife, but simply refer to one item, that is to say that there are a number of things which polite people now eat at the dinner table with their fingers and never use a fork with them.

The Chicago Herald gives these directions. Lettuce is to be taken up in the fingers and should be dipped in the dressing or a little salt. Celery may be properly placed on the table alongside the plate. Strawberries when served with stems on, as they usually are now, at the more fashionable tables. Bread, toast and all tarts and small cakes. Fruit of all kinds, except melons and preserves, both of which are eaten with a spoon. Cheese is now almost invariably taken up with the fingers. The legs or other small pieces of a bird are handled with the fingers at fashionable dinners, and at most of the stylish luncheons, the ladies pick up small pieces of chicken without using a fork.

Responsibilities of the Hour

With the late call for 100,000 men for one hundred days service, new responsibilities devolve upon the husbandman, already self-taxed with a large amount of work laid out for himself and little help. This little in many instances is taken from him and now the only help is to put the brain actively at work and make that help the hands and save the heels. This can be done in many instances in the better planning of the work to be done.

Have a map or plat of the farm made out, unless you can keep all in your mind with memoranda of each crop growing, when planted, progress, condition, &c. and put the labor upon such parts as will tell the best for it. Much labor and time will be saved by having the ground well and thoroughly prepared for the crop, even if you have to confine your operations to fewer acres.

Every dollar of money or time expended in the proper preparation of the ground will save double the amount in after culture in all hoed crops; especially will this be the case in field corn. There, as soon as the crop is up or about coming up, run a harrow over the rows lengthwise. The weeds can thus be kept down until the corn obtains a good start. Then it can be worked by the improved cultivators by the young or old members of the family.

A field properly prepared and cared for in time will be sure to yield an amount paying a very large percent over that as ordinarily tilled. Every advantage will be taken of improved machinery as now obtainable, but much caution should be exercised in selecting to obtain such as is worthy and will be found to answer the purpose, without constantly running to the shops to repair. If you have not them, get a kit of tools, augurs, planes, saws, hammers &c. with an assortment of nails and screws, which should always be at hand for repairing or making any simple contrivance wanted without be obliged to waste precious time.

Remember that every bushel of grain that can be grown will be wanted to supply the demand that is sure to come. Put in a variety not confining your crops to one kind.

Editor's note:

I think it is worth noting that, in the midst of the Civil War, *Prairie Farmer* brought its readers practical suggestions to help them carry on with daily activities in times of stress and uncertainty. The magazine stated clearly that "every bushel of grain," every individual effort, is important. What timeless advice.

CHAPTER SEVEN

Cookies & Desserts

This chapter, perhaps more than any other, indicates the state of life among the readers of *Prairie Farmer* magazine. I can almost measure the progress in women's leisure time and improvements in kitchen equipment by the number of cookie recipes each year.

> *"For dessert . . . Farmer's Rice Pudding. The man that would not put up with that should take a trip to California by the overland route."*
> **Prairie Farmer, December 1851**

Puddings, as our pioneer cooks knew them, were a carryover from the earliest days of our country, and the preparation is opposite that of cookies. The term pudding almost always refers to a dense cake-like dish. Most frequently the batter was wrapped in a tightly woven "pudding cloth" and immersed in boiling water for two or three hours. As the century progressed, puddings were steamed in large kettles and even baked. I've started to make my steamed puddings in the microwave. Try experimenting yourself with some of the unedited recipes we've included in this chapter.

There are very few cookie recipes in the first 15 years. By the late 1880s, there are quite a few. Cookies are virtually impossible to make on a hearth with a small reflector oven. Few of those came with flat sheets for baking and when they did, they were quite small. The pioneer housewife could bake only six cookies at a time.

Unlike cakes or pies, which the frontier homemaker could put in the oven for a half hour or more while she did other chores, cookies required constant attention. They bake quickly and the sheets needed rotation to bake evenly. The January 26, 1886, article on Children's Lunches provides a some late-century opinions on cooking treats.

Like cookies, custards are very challenging to make on a hearth or poorly controlled stove. We don't see too many recipes for egg and milk custards until the 1860s and '70s. The inclusion of ice cream recipes is another indicator of farming improvements. After all, you can't make ice cream unless you have ice. Ice in the summer is expensive to purchase unless you have your own icehouse.

Basic Cookies

 **Editor's note:**

This very early cookie recipe uses just the basics. They are simple and not too sweet. They make a nice complement to a glass of milk or cup of coffee. To fancy them up for tea, the farm wife might spread a bit of tart plum or raspberry jam on the bottom of one cookie and sandwich it with a second.

1 cup butter
3 cups firmly packed brown sugar
3 eggs
5 cups flour
1 teaspoon baking soda
1 cup milk
2 cups chopped nuts (optional)

Preheat the oven to 350 degrees F. Cream the butter and sugar until fluffy. Add the eggs and mix well. Stir in half the flour and the baking soda. Mix until smooth. Gently stir in the milk and when combined add the remaining flour. Stir in the nuts if desired. Drop by teaspoons on a lightly greased cookie sheet. Bake until the tops are a golden brown, 8 to12 minutes. Cookies puff up while baking and sink a bit as they cool.

DECEMBER 1851

Farmer's Rice Pudding

1/4 cup uncooked rice
(not instant or converted)
1/4 cup brown sugar, firmly packed
2 cups milk

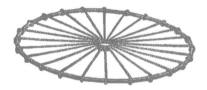

Combine the ingredients in a microwavable container. One that has a wide, flat bottom works best, so as to allow the most milk to come in contact with the rice and sugar. Microwave for 5 minutes at 1/3 power, open and stir. Continue microwaving at 1/3 power and stirring in 5-minute inetervals until the milk is absorbed and the rice is tender. This may take 1/2 hour or longer. The original recipe called for baking in the oven and stirring from time to time for 3 hours. Serve warm or cold.

Cookies without Eggs

1 cup sugar
1/2 cup butter
1 teaspoon baking soda
1/2 teaspoon cinnamon
2 3/4 cups flour
1/2 cup cold water

Preheat the oven to 350 degrees F. Cream the butter and sugar. Add the baking soda, cinnamon and half the flour. Mix in the cold water and then the remaining flour. The dough will be quite stiff; you may want to knead in the last of the flour by hand. On a well-floured surface, roll out the dough very thin, almost as though you can see through it. Cut into squares or use decorative cutters and cut into shapes. Place on lightly greased cookie sheets. Bake 10 minutes or until lightly browned.

Soft Cookies

Editor's note:

Caraway seeds were a common early cookie flavoring. The combination of sweet and savory gives these treats a sophisticated taste.

2 cups cream
2 cups sugar
3 eggs
4 cups flour
2 teaspoons baking soda
2 teaspoons caraway seeds
Note: Butter is not used in this recipe.

Preheat oven to 350 degrees F. Combine the cream, sugar and eggs in a large mixing bowl. Stir in the flour, baking soda and caraway seeds. Drop by teaspoons onto a lightly greased cookie sheet. Bake until the cookie is set and just beginning to brown around the edges, about 12 minutes.

Gingersnaps

January 6, 1859
All railroads running to
fashionable watering places
during the summer are
trunk lines.

*Boil together 2 heaping tablespoons ginger, 2
coffee cups sorghum. Add 14 tablespoons melted
butter, cool but not cold, 1 tablespoon sugar,
1 1/2 teaspoons soda, 3 pints flour. Roll, then
bake in a slow oven.*
—A subscriber from Fremont in Tazwell
County, Ill.

OCTOBER 10, 1877

Chocolate Macaroons

2 egg whites
1/2 cup sugar
2 tablespoons flour
1/2 teaspoon baking powder
4 tablespoons cocoa

Preheat the oven to 325 degrees F. In a
perfectly clean bowl with grease-free beaters,
whip the egg whites until they form stiff
peaks. Combine the dry ingredients and fold
into the egg whites. Drop by teaspoons onto
an ungreased baking sheet. Bake until the
cookies are dry and firm, about 15 minutes.
Watch closely so they don't burn. Store in a
tightly sealed container.

Cheap Cookies

2 cups sugar
1 cup lard
(you can substitute butter or margarine)
2 teaspoons baking powder
6 cups flour
1 cup milk
Note: Eggs are not used in this recipe.

Preheat the oven to 350 degrees F. Cream the lard and sugar. Add the baking powder and half the flour, mixing well. Stir in the milk and the rest of the flour. The dough will be quite stiff. Roll out fairly thin on a lightly floured surface. Cut into shapes and bake on a lightly greased cookie sheet until light brown, about 10 minutes.

JANUARY 26, 1886

Ginger Cookies — *Children's Lunches*

I think nearly all little folks enjoy more variety in the school meal than we are apt to suppose, and I never think it time lost to make it as palatable as possible. I have known many a child who, tired from long confinement in a close schoolroom, needed some tempting morsel to stimulate the appetite and otherwise would let the dinner go untouched. There is a great sameness in a dinner day after day of just bread and butter and perhaps a bit of cold meat that is often tough and tasteless. So while I would not advise giving children a great variety, thoughtfulness in this direction is desirable. If "variety" is the "spice of life," it is so to hungry boys and girls.

—Mrs. Harris

I have to get up luncheons five days a week for my four hungry children as they all go to school, and they always relish molasses cookies. I use 2 cups of molasses or one of molasses and one of brown sugar, 3/4 cup lard or half lard and half butter, 1 cup of hot water, a teaspoon each of soda and ginger, a little salt and lastly a half teaspoon powdered alum. Mix in flour soft as can be rolled and bake in a quick oven. I do not think so little alum can be harmful, while it improves the cookies.

—Mrs. Smart

I well remember when I went to school how much I enjoyed sharing in the lunch of my seat mate, even though it was prepared much plainer than my own. The seasoned doughnuts and tough pies seasoned with allspice, relished occasionally more than the sweetened crullers, and nice pastry. It was a change everyone craves in even so small a matter as a child's lunch.

—Mrs. Jones

I find little time to make cakes for my children's lunches, but I take pains to have plenty of good bread and butter, cold meat and fruit also as we now have plenty of it. I keep cake as a sort of luxury for them to resort to when they seem to need a change; and as for pies, I rarely make them, unless it be really simple ones occasionally.

—Mrs. Lealand

About Simple Food

In the matter of cooking, it is not usually the housekeeper's fault that it is not as simple and of a little variety as possible. Who are the first to complain of simple meals, but the heads of our houses and who can blame them?

I had a small trial of giving our farmers a boarding house breakfast of cracked wheat or oatmeal, etc., a city lunch of whatever came handy and a light digestible country tea. Every member of the family, from grandfather to the smallest of the household was in rebellion, and even the girl hired then threatened to desert if we didn't live better. Why even the cats were so disgusted by the scraps from the table that they gathered their tails about them and forever shook

the dust of our premises from their feet. With such a civil war pending over me, weakened in spirit and body by such frugal diet, I was only too glad to come back to our old-time substantial diet.

It may do for delicate women and growing children, but for real muscular labor, there is nothing that goes right to the spot like a dish of Boston Baked Beans and a generous slice of pie or something equally substantial. So says the head of this house, and according to the household, so must the woman cook. I find recipes for food that will "keep" of great help. Take half a day and bake a lot of Gingersnaps and Keeping Cookies.
—*Clara Francis*

Jumbles

When I was a child I used to think my mother's jumbles the best possible cakes that could be made. Here is her recipe. They are richer than some may like, but they are good nonetheless and will keep a long time.

—*Mrs. Dyer*

3/4 cup sugar
3/4 cup butter
3 eggs
1 teaspoon baking soda
1/2 teaspoon nutmeg
3 or 4 cups flour

Preheat the oven to 350 degrees F. Cream the butter and sugar. Add the eggs and beat well. Stir in the baking soda and nutmeg and the flour. You want dough that is not sticky, but that can still be molded. Knead the dough briefly and then form the cookies into the traditional doughnut shape. Take a small ball of dough and make it into a long pencil-like length. Bring the two ends together and seal them. Dip the top of the cookie into some sugar and place on a lightly greased cookie sheet. Bake until the cookies are just beginning to brown, about 10 minutes.

Keeping Cookies

These cookies will keep many weeks if made this way.

3 cups sugar
1 cup butter
2 eggs
1 1/2 teaspoon baking soda
2 cups sour cream
1/2 teaspoon nutmeg
5 cups flour, or enough so you can
roll the dough out nicely

Preheat the oven to 350 degrees F. Cream the butter and sugar. Beat in the eggs. Add the baking soda and nutmeg and 1/2 the flour. Stir in the sour cream. Add the remaining flour until the dough is very stiff. Divide and roll out 1/2 inch thick on a lightly floured surface. Cut into squares or shapes and place on a lightly greased cookie sheet. Bake until lightly browned and firm in the center, about 15 minutes. Store in a tightly sealed container.

Gingersnaps

1 cups sugar
1 cup lard, or butter or margarine
1 cup molasses
1 tablespoon ginger
1 teaspoon baking soda
4 cups flour, you may need more

Preheat the oven to 325 degrees F. Cream the sugar and fat; stir in the molasses, ginger and baking soda. Begin adding the flour 1 cup at a time until you have a dough that is stiff and not sticky. Form the dough into small balls, about 1/2 inch in diameter. Roll the balls in granulated sugar and place on a lightly greased cookie sheet. Press the dough flat with a glass dipped in sugar. Bake until the edges begin to brown, about 10 minutes. Watch carefully; they can burn easily.

Sweet Potato Pudding

1/2 pound cooked sweet potatoes, grated
6 ounces sugar
6 ounces butter
6 egg yolks
Peel and juice of a lemon
1/2 cup wine
I teaspoon nutmeg
6 stiff egg whites

Preheat the oven to 325 degrees F. Combine the sweet potatoes, sugar, butter, egg yolks, lemon and nutmeg. Fold in the egg whites gently. Put into a lightly greased casserole dish and bake until the pudding is set. Serve warm with a sweet sauce. The cooking time varies greatly with the size and shape of your baking dish.

JUNE 23, 1875

Strawberry Ice Cream

Editor's note:

This strawberry ice cream recipe is a particular favorite of our family; we set our two grandsons to cranking the freezer every July Fourth.

1 quart fresh strawberries
1 1/4 cups sugar
Another 1 1/4 cups sugar
1 quart cream
1 pint additional strawberries, finely chopped

Crush the strawberries with a masher or in a food processor and combine with the first 1 1/4 cups sugar. Set aside for at least 3 hours, or overnight. Drain the berries through a fine sieve, saving the juice and discarding the remaining berry bits. Add the second 1 1/4 cups sugar and mix until it is dissolved. Stir in the cream and put in the freezer compartment of the refrigerator to pre-freeze. Add the last pint of berries and complete the freezing process in an ice cream freezer. This makes about 2 quarts of ice cream. Check the capacity of your ice cream freezer and process in 2 batches if necessary.

Apple Pudding

6 small baking apples
2 cups sifted flour
1 1/2 cups milk
1/2 cup whipping cream
4 eggs

Preheat the oven to 350 degrees F. Peel apples and take out core without cutting the apple into pieces. Arrange the apples in a lightly greased baking dish large enough to hold them in one layer with the batter, but not too large. Mix the batter very smooth and pour over the apples. Bake until the batter is set, about 1 hour.

MAY 17, 1860

Lemon Ice Cream

3 egg yolks
1 quart milk
1 cup sugar
1 pint cream
Yellow peels only of 2 lemons
cut into thin strips
Note: Reserve lemons for another purpose.

Combine all ingredients in a large saucepan. Heat over moderate to low heat, stirring until the mixture comes to a boil. Lower the heat and simmer for 10 minutes, stirring frequently. Set aside to cool. Remove the lemon peels and pre-freeze the mixture in your refrigerator freezer compartment. Finish processing in an ice cream freezer.

Cherry Pudding and Sweet Sauces

Make a light dough as for tea biscuit; roll it out in a long narrow strip. Have ready a bowl of stoned cherries. Strew them thickly over the dough; dust a little flour over them and roll up, loosely pinching the edges and ends together. Flour a cloth lightly; wrap it loosely around the roll and put it into a steamer over boiling water and steam it about an hour, more or less, according to its size.

Make a sauce of 1 pint of boiling water, 1 teacup sugar and 2 tablespoons butter, thickened with a little cornstarch and flavored with extract of lemon. When done, stir into it the well-beaten white of an egg. Sweetened cream flavored with nutmeg is also nice for a sauce, as is butter and sugar rubbed to a cream and flavored as preferred.

—*Mrs. Peters*

JUNE 15, 1886

Strawberry Shortcake

5 eggs, separated
2 cups sugar
4 tablespoons water
Juice of 1 lemon
2 teaspoons baking powder
4 cups sifted flour

Preheat the oven to 350 degrees F. Beat together the egg yolks and sugar until thick and lemon colored. Combine the water and lemon juice. Add the baking soda to 2 cups of the flour and stir into the batter. Add the liquid and then the rest of the flour. In a perfectly clean bowl with grease-free beaters, whip the egg whites until they form stiff peaks. Fold into the batter. Spread the batter about 1/4 inch thick on greased and floured jellyroll pans. It will make two to four pans, depending upon size. Bake until the cake is firm, about 20 minutes. Cut into squares, sandwich with fresh strawberries and, as the original recipe said, "As this dish is served pour cream over it. The more liberal the supply of cream the more relishable will be the cake."

Sour Sauce

2 cups molasses
1 cup water
1/2 cup vinegar
2 eggs
2 tablespoons butter

Combine the molasses, water and vinegar in a medium saucepan. Stir in the eggs and bring to a boil gradually. Cook, stirring constantly, until thickened, about 10 minutes. Stir in the butter.

JUNE 16, 1883

Vinegar Sauce

1 1/2 cups sugar
1 1/2 tablespoons flour
1/4 teaspoon nutmeg
2 tablespoons vinegar
1 1/2 pints boiling water
1 teaspoon butter

Combine the sugar, flour and nutmeg in a medium-sized saucepan. Stir in the vinegar and water. Bring to a boil, reduce heat and simmer for 10 minutes. Stir in the butter and serve over puddings or cakes.

JULY 24, 1886

Raspberry Pudding

For a small family, put a pint of the berries into a pudding dish; strew over them a few breadcrumbs and half a teacup of sugar. Make a crust as for nice tea biscuits but soft enough to be stirred with a spoon; spread it evenly over the berries and bake in a moderate oven or, if preferable, steam it until done. To be eaten with a hot sauce or creamed butter and sugar as liked .
—Mrs. Newell

A pudding that always meets with favor at our table is made of the red berries. First pre-pare a custard from a quart of milk, the yolks of four eggs and whites of two, one pint of bread crumbs, sugar to taste and a piece of butter the size of an egg. Flavor with vanilla and bake.

When done, spread with a thick layer of sugared berries. Make a meringue by beating the whites to a froth, adding 3 tablespoons of sugar and 1/2 teaspoon lemon extract. Spread this over the berries, return it to the oven and bake to a light brown. This is best eaten soon after baked.
—Mrs. Everts

Peach Melange

June 6, 1888
A lady who advertised for a girl to do "light housework" received a letter from an applicant who said her health demanded sea air and who wondered where the lighthouse was located.

A good dessert dish is prepared thus: Pour one pint of boiling milk over 3/4 pound of bread crumbs. Add 1/2 cupful of sugar, a large tablespoon of butter and 3 well-beaten eggs. Flavor with 20 drops of extract of almond. In the bottom of a well-buttered pudding mold, put one pint of peach jam or the same amount of canned peaches. Pour the mixture over this fruit and cover closely. Steam two hours.

—Mrs. Hubbard

JULY 14, 1888

Tutti Frutti

Editor's note:

This method works well to dress up purchased ice cream. You want a premium-quality ice cream with a high butterfat and low air content. Soften it slightly in the microwave or refrigerator. Stir in the fresh or dried fruit and re-freeze in a plastic reclosable container. Stir once or twice during the refreezing process to help distribute the fruits evenly.

This is a very nice change from ordinary ice cream. When the cream is partially frozen, add candied fruits of any kind as chopped citron and raisins or fresh peaches, cherries or berries, using about as much fruit in quantity as there is cream.

—Mrs Strong

Macaroni Pudding

4 ounces macaroni or spaghetti
3 cups milk
1/2 cup half and half
3 tablespoons butter
1/3 cup sugar
3 eggs

Preheat the oven to 350 degrees F. If using spaghetti, break it into 1-inch pieces. Combine the pasta with the milk in a large saucepan. Bring to a boil, lower the heat and simmer until the pasta is very, very tender and much of the liquid has been absorbed. Be sure to stir this as it cooks to prevent the pasta from sticking to the bottom of the pot. Cool slightly and add the butter, sugar and well-beaten eggs. Pour into a lightly greased casserole and bake until the pudding is set in the center, about 45 minutes.

Delicate Indian Pudding

1 quart milk
1/2 cup corn meal
4 tablespoon sugar
1/2 teaspoon ginger
1 tablespoon soft butter
3 eggs

Preheat the oven to 325 degrees F. Boil the milk and sprinkle in the corn meal, stirring all the while. Cook for 15 minutes. Beat together the sugar, ginger, butter and eggs. Stir into the cooked corn meal. Pour into a greased casserole and bake until a knife put in the center comes out clean, about 1 hour. Serve with a sweet or vinegar sauce.

CHAPTER EIGHT

Cakes

Working with these cake recipes is an adventure and an education. In the earliest recipes, all the authors provide is a listing of ingredients, recognizing that the readers of *Prairie Farmer* knew "the rule" for baking cakes. Some of these ingredient names need to be interpreted. For example, "saleratus" is an early form of baking soda. Measurements frequently require interpretation as well, "butter the size of an egg," "flour to make stiff as biscuits," and "gill" can be confounding.

"Spice to taste" is another direction used frequently. Chocolate was rare and, in fact, most recipes called "chocolate cake" are yellow cake with chocolate icing or filling. Vanilla was just as rare. The seed pod of a wild orchid found in Mexico, vanilla extract did not began to appear in recipes until the middle of the 1880s. Common cake flavorings were nutmeg and lemon — using fresh juice and peel or extract. Spice cakes, made by blending together a number of aromatic spices, were favorites, as was gingerbread. There are scores of recipes for gingerbread. They range

> *"The most difficult of the young housewife's duties is that of baking . . . . It is a matter of guesswork after all."*
> **Prairie Farmer, January 15, 1877**

from the very early ones, which are baked like bars and crisp cookies on sheets or jelly roll pans, to a square cake like the ones we bake today. The pioneers valued ginger as an aid to digestion, so having plain gingerbread set back in the pantry was considered useful as a remedy for touchy stomachs.

Baking pan sizes and temperatures were also often left to the cook to determine. As you work with these recipes, feel free to use any pan you prefer. You will find a lot of references to loaf cakes. And if you have a flair for the authentic, turban-shaped pans are still available in antique shops. Just remember, if you are baking in an angel food or bundt pan, lower the oven temperature and bake longer.

I hope you enjoy working with these recipes. You will find the cakes are denser and less sweet than today's cakes. They keep well, frozen or in the refrigerator. I've found myself delighted on more than one occasion to do as our pioneer predecessors did and go back into the larder to bring out new favorite cake for company.

Baking

The most difficult of the young housewife's duties is that of baking. Food prepared in the best manner may be ruined by a fire that is either too hot, or too slow, during any part of the process. . . . It is a matter of guesswork after all. In fact our whole system of cooking is more or less a patched up system of guesswork. We have rules and recipes for rich cakes and puddings, but bread of all varieties, pies, butter &c. are made by guess.

And even in those recipes which we have, the ingredients are measured in all manner of vessels, and no two persons understand alike the terms which designate the quantities. One of my friends had a stove with glass oven doors. Why could not a thermometer also be attached to them?

I hope to see the time when cooking shall become an exact science: when we shall not only measure the heat of our ovens with thermometers and know the precise temperature of which they should be for each variety baked therein, but shall also know the temperature at which our yeast and bread-sponge and cream should be kept, when we shall prepare all articles of food by correct recipes and measure all ingredients in exact and standard measures, which shall be alike all over the country, so that mistakes can only occur when we fail to follow the rules.

—Mrs. Rosetta B. Hastings,
Atchison County, Kan.

Editor's note:

The two very early cake recipes on the following page illustrate the challenges in working with historic recipes. I am showing the original and the way I have interpreted it. By looking at other 19th-century recipes in *Prairie Farmer* and other cookbooks of the period, I am able to make an educated guess as to the quantities of the unmeasured ingredients. I continue to be surprised by the wonderful tastes that we have forgotten. It makes the extra effort, and the occasional failures before the recipe is perfected, worthwhile.

August 26, 1883
Flowers are the
sweetest things
that God ever
made and forgot
to put a soul into.

Gingerloaf

2 cups molasses, 2 cups buttermilk, 1 teaspoon soda, 4 eggs, flour, ginger and spices to taste.

2 cups molasses
2 cups buttermilk
4 eggs, separated
3 cups flour
1 teaspoon soda

Spices to taste
2 tablespoons ginger
1 teaspoon cinnamon
1/4 teaspoon cloves

Preheat oven to 325 degrees F. In a large mixing bowl combine the molasses, buttermilk and egg yolks. Beat well. Stir in the flour, soda and spices. In a clean bowl with grease-free beaters, whip the egg whites until they form stiff peaks. Fold them into the cake batter. Grease and flour two standard-size loaf pans. Divide batter between them. Bake until a tester put in the center of the loaf comes out clean, about 1 hour.

Wisconsin Sponge Cake

Eggs, 1 teacup buttermilk, 1 teaspoon salt, 2 tablespoons cream. Stir to consistency of pancake batter. Bake 20 minutes on pie ties and eat while hot with butter.

3 eggs
1 cup buttermilk
1 teaspoon salt (optional)
2 tablespoons heavy cream
1 1/2 cups flour

Preheat oven to 375 degrees F. Stir the liquid ingredients together. Add the flour and pour into two 8-inch pie tins. Bake 20 minutes.

Editor's note:

This cake bakes up very light and filled with air, almost like a large popover. I am not at all sure this is the way it is supposed to turn out, but it is very tasty and, as the original says, good to eat hot with butter.

Ginger Bread

3 cups flour
1 tablespoon baking soda
2 tablespoons ginger
1 tablespoon cinnamon
1 cup cold butter
1 cup molasses
2 eggs
1/4 cup milk

Editor's note:

This very early gingerbread is similar to Colonial recipes. It is more like a cookie and has an almost dry texture. The Soft Gingerbread recipe that follows is from the middle of the century and is much more like the cake we eat today.

Preheat the oven to 350 degrees F. Combine the dry ingredients. Cut in the butter as for pie crust. Stir in the molasses, eggs and milk to form a very stiff dough. Roll out 1/2 inch thick on a lightly floured surface. Cut into squares or shapes and bake on a greased cookie sheet until firm and light brown, 10 to 15 minutes.

MAY 5, 1877

Soft Gingerbread

1 cup dark molasses
1/2 cup firmly packed brown sugar
1/2 cup butter
1 teaspoon ground ginger
1 egg
1/2 cup sour milk (or buttermilk)
2 1/2 cups flour
2 teaspoons baking soda
1/3 cup hot tap water

Preheat oven to 325 degrees F. In a medium saucepan combine the molasses, brown sugar and butter. Heat until just boiling, remove from heat and let cool. Add the ginger, egg, milk and flour and mix well. Carefully add the baking soda to the hot water. It will bubble up. Then add the dissolved soda to the batter. Bake in five mini loaf pans for 45 minutes or until the center is firm.

Cake Baking by a Baker

Alfred L. Winans,
Hancock County, Ill., writes:

I will try and show the reason why so many recipes are abortive in the hands of our women. In the first place, different lots of flour, sugar, molasses, butter &c. seldom are precisely alike in their quantities. Eggs differ in size as well as quality — bakers, in speaking of eggs, mean that the size that will require nine for a pound, the 10th egg being allowed for the weight of the shell. The tougher the flour, the greater is this tendency to spring — as it is technically called. This property must always be borne in mind, and when the flour is short in its nature, a little more must be added to the quantity in the recipe. Sugar differs in its dryness, also in its saccharine properties. When moist, use less liquid, when very rich or dry, use more.

With these premises after all, nothing but judgement and experience will make a complete cake baker. Observe, when baking cakes, that sometimes, if they have room, they will run over the tin sheet and become shapeless; at other items, the same recipe will contract in circumference and rise up furiously in the middle. In the first instance, there is too much saccharine or sugar. The remedy: more water or flour or both. In the last instance, the defect is the contrary. Therefore, the obvious remedy is more sugar —sometimes more butter — but in most cases the sugar will remedy.

When a cake dough is mixed, press the finger on it. If the impress remains lifeless without following the finger somewhat when removed, it is too rich. Add flour and, if useful, work in a little water. If it follows the removal of the finger with alacrity, it is not light enough and will contract in baking. You want the happy medium between spreading and drawing up. Your cake should run just as much as the lightening of the saleratus will cause it and no more.

Batters you must lift on a paddle or spoon. If it drops off short, it is too rich. It must be like the dough, a small degree of toughness. It will take observation to become an expert, but it can be very readily acquired by any who feels interested, will note the qualities and feeling of their mixtures before each baking, and will experiment on small portions of the same batch that they have in hand at the time. Do not be discouraged at a failure at first, but persevere, and you will be able to tell with certainty the fault, if any, in any recipe that comes in your way and improve the most of them.

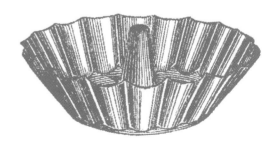

Economizing Time

It requires no little effort on my part to find time during the summer months for more than the most cursory reading as our farm work is constant and exhausting, but I am learning in this and in many other things, "Where there is a will there is a way." I cannot be sufficiently thankful for the lessons of perseverance received from my excellent mother. She taught me when a very little child to finish whatever was begun as soon as practicable. If it was hemming a dish-cloth, or knitting an allotted task, or piecing patchwork, she had me finish it before beginning anything else of the kind.

Many persons have a great variety of work on hand and wait for the "spirit to move" for their completion. This habit of doing a thing or not as one feels inclined, leads to much thriftlessness and inefficiency. Parents who let their children stay away from school because they want a change or are tired of their hum-drum duties are culti-vating the same lax habit in them and sooner or later both will feel the bad effects.

—Mrs. Wise

This habit of doing exactly what is to be done in each hour, is all-important, but how few of us are practicing it. In work, for instance, how often we are interrupted and the hour is filled very differently from what we had planned. It is well, however, to have an ideal, and to come as near it as possible, for those who are prompt enough to use all their time profitably, gathering up the minutes that many thoughtlessly waste, may be said to have made that much extra time. I do not believe, however, in all work. In these summer days, let us each contrive some rest and healthful recreation, not forgetting to fill in as much instructive reading as possible, that the mind may not stagnate or remain stationary.

—Mrs. Walter

MARCH 1851

Providence Cake

Below I offer you some recipes for cakes I know to have been repeatedly baked and proved excellent. I think 1 1/2 cup rich cream is better than milk and butter. —A Prairie Farmer reader

5 eggs, separated
3 cups firmly packed brown sugar
1 1/2 cups whipping cream
or 1 cup butter and 1 cup milk
1/2 teaspoon soda
5 cups flour

Preheat the oven to 350 degrees F. Mix the brown sugar and whipping cream and beat well. Add the egg yolks. Stir in the baking soda and gradually add the flour. Whip the egg whites until stiff peaks form. Fold them into the cake batter. Grease and flour a 9- by 12-inch pan. Bake about 45 minutes, or until firm in center and slightly pulled away from sides.

Cake Without Eggs

Had this been in the February number, it would have been good for the trial by people living in town where eggs have been 50 cents a dozen. More such recipes will be accepted. —The Prairie Farmer editor

1/2 cup butter
2 cups firmly packed brown sugar
1 cup cream
1 cup buttermilk
4 cups flour
2 teaspoon baking soda
1 teaspoon cinnamon
1/2 teaspoon nutmeg
1/2 teaspoon mace
1 cup currants

Preheat oven to 325 degrees F. Cream the butter add the sugar and gradually add the cream and buttermilk. Stir in the flour and spices. Add the currants last. Pour batter into a well-greased bundt or tube pan. Bake from 1 1/2 to 1 3/4 hours.

Cup Cake

Editor's note:

The original recipe called for double the amount of spices. This is one of those occasions when I wonder if the original *Prairie Farmer* proofreader was paying attention. But even with the reduced spices, it is nice to have a small cake that packs a spicy wallop.

1 1/4 cups firmly packed brown sugar
1/2 cup butter
2 eggs
1 egg white
1 1/4 cup molasses
1/2 cup buttermilk
1 1/2 teaspoons baking soda
3 cups flour
2 tablespoons ginger
2 tablespoons cloves
2 tablespoons allspice

Preheat the oven to 350 degrees F. Cream the sugar and butter. Add the molasses, eggs and egg white, beating well. Mix the remaining dry ingredients together. Add half the flour mixture, the buttermilk and then the remaining flour, stirring well after each addition. Grease and flour cupcake or gem pans. Bake until firm, about 25 minutes for cupcakes and 20 for gem pans.

Imitation Sponge Cake

2 cups sugar
1/12 cup butter
3 eggs
1/2 cup milk
1/2 cup cold water
3 cups flour
2 teaspoons cream of tartar
1 teaspoon baking soda
mace, nutmeg or lemon to taste

Preheat oven to 350 degrees F. Cream the butter and sugar. Add the eggs one at a time and beat well. Sift together the flour, cream of tartar and baking soda. Set aside. Add the flavoring of your choice, 1/2 teaspoon mace or nutmeg or 1 teaspoon lemon extract to the batter. Add 1/3 of the flour mixture, then the milk, another 1/3 of the flour, the cold water and finally the last 1/3 of the flour. Lightly grease and flour 2 standard loaf pans. Divide the batter between them. Bake until the center is firm to the touch and a skewer put in the center comes out clean, about 45 minutes.

Temperance Cake

3 eggs
2 cups firmly packed brown sugar
1 cup milk
1 teaspoon baking soda
1 teaspoon nutmeg
2 cups flour

Preheat the oven to 350 degrees F. Beat the eggs and sugar together until thick, this may take five or more minutes. Combine the flour, baking soda and nutmeg. Add half of the flour mixture to the batter, then the milk, followed by the rest of the flour. Lightly grease and flour a 10- by 15-inch jellyroll pan. Pour the batter in and spread smooth. Bake until firm to the touch and lightly browned, about 20 minutes. You can spread this cake with a tart jelly and roll it up as a jelly roll, or simply cut and serve as bars.

Silver Cake

1 cup sugar
1/2 cup butter
1 1/2 cup flour
1 teaspoon cream of tartar
1/2 teaspoon baking soda
1 teaspoon lemon extract
4 egg whites, whipped

Editor's Note:

These companion cakes, Silver Cake and Gold Cake, split the eggs — the whites in the silver cake and the yolks in the gold. Bake both and alternate layers with a white frosting.

Preheat the oven to 350 degrees F. Cream the butter and sugar. Combine the flour, cream of tartar and baking soda. Stir into the batter. Add the lemon extract. Fold in the whipped egg whites. Lightly grease and flour two round cake pans. Divide the batter between them. Bake until firm in the center and slightly pulled away from the sides, about 35 minutes.

Gold Cake

1 cup firmly packed brown sugar
1/2 cup butter
4 egg yolks
1/2 cup milk
1 1/2 cup flour
1 teaspoon cream of tartar
1/2 teaspoon soda
1/2 teaspoon nutmeg

Preheat the oven to 350 degrees F. Cream the butter and sugar. Add the egg yolks and beat well. Combine the flour, cream of tartar, baking soda and nutmeg. Stir in half the flour mixture, then the milk and finally the last of the flour mixture. Lightly grease and flour two round cake pans. Divide the batter between them. Bake until firm in the center and slightly pulled away from the sides, about 35 minutes.

APRIL 20, 1867

Cropper Cake

1/2 cup butter
1/2 cup firmly packed brown sugar
1/2 cup molasses
2 eggs, separated
1/2 cup milk
2 cups flour
1 teaspoon cinnamon

Preheat the oven to 350 degrees F. Cream the butter and brown sugar. Stir in the molasses and egg yolks. Add the cinnamon and half the flour. Stir in the milk and then the remaining flour. In a clean bowl with grease-free beaters, whip the egg whites until stiff peaks form. Fold them into the cake batter. Pour batter into a standard loaf pan. Bake until firm in the center, about 50 minutes.

FEBRUARY 18, 1871

Custard Cake

2 cups firmly packed brown sugar
1/2 cup butter
3 eggs
1 teaspoon baking soda
2 teaspoons cream of tartar
3 cups flour

For the custard:
1 cup milk
4 tablespoons sugar
1 tablespoon corn starch
3 lightly beaten eggs
1 pound chopped walnuts or almonds

Preheat the oven to 350 degrees F. Cream the butter and sugar. Beat in the eggs. Sift together the flour, baking soda and cream of tartar. Gradually add to the butter mixture. Grease and flour four 8- or 9-inch round cake pans. Divide the batter among the pans and bake until lightly browned, about 20 minutes. Cool in pans for five minutes and then continue cooling on cake racks. Fill with custard.

Combine the cornstarch and sugar. Stir in the milk and eggs. Bring to a boil, lower the heat and simmer, stirring, until the custard is thickened. Cool the custard and stir in the nuts. Fill between cooled cake layers and store in the refrigerator. You may want to run skewers through the layers to keep them from sliding.

Note: When first baked, the cake is a bit dry. After filling, the custard is partially absorbed and the whole becomes deliciously creamy.

Cream Sponge Cake

2 eggs
Cream to fill up a 1-cup measure
1 cup sugar
1 cup flour
2 teaspoons baking powder
1 teaspoon lemon extract

Preheat the oven to 350 degrees F. Lightly beat the two eggs in a 1-cup measuring cup. Add cream to make 1 cup. Combine this mixture with sugar and beat well. Sift the flour and baking powder. Fold into the sugar-egg mixture. Stir in the lemon extract. Grease and flour a 9-inch layer cake pan. Pour in the batter. Bake until light brown, for 20 to 25 minutes.

Fairy Cake

1/2 cup butter
1 cup sugar
1/2 cup milk
1/2 cup corn starch
1/2 teaspoon baking soda
1 1/2 cups flour
1 teaspoon cream of tartar
4 stiffly beaten egg whites
2 drops red food coloring

Editor's note:

The original recipe calls for making six alternating pink and white layers. There are only three cups of batter, so this must have been originally made in a small turban mold. If you have such a pan, it would be a very nice way to use it. A number of cake recipes used cornstarch as part of the dry ingredients. It makes a very delicate cake, somewhat dryer than cakes made with flour alone.

Preheat the oven to 350 degrees F. Cream the butter and sugar. Sift together cornstarch, baking soda, flour and cream of tartar. Stir half the dry ingredients into the creamed mixture, then the milk and finally the rest of the dry ingredients. Fold in the beaten egg whites. Take 1/3 of the cake batter and color it with the red food coloring. Grease and flour either a loaf pan or a 9-inch round pan. If using the loaf pan, put in half the white batter, drop in the pink and cover with the remaining white. Run a knife through to marbleize the cake. If using the round layer, alternate white batter with pink and similarly run the knife through. Bake 35 to 45 minutes until just light brown and firm in the middle.

Jelly Cake

1 1/2 cups firmly packed brown sugar
1/2 cup butter
3 eggs, separated
1/2 cup buttermilk
1/2 teaspoon baking soda
2 cups flour

Preheat the oven to 350 degrees F. Butter and flour three 8- or 9-inch round cake pans. Cream the butter and sugar. Stir in the egg yolks, reserving the whites. Stir in the baking soda and 1 cup of the flour. Add the buttermilk and mix well. Add the rest of the flour. Beat the egg whites with grease-free beaters in a clean bowl. Fold into the cake batter. Divide the batter among the cake pans. You will have 3 thin layers.

Bake until firm in the center, about 20 minutes. Cool in the pans for 5 minutes then finish cooling on cake racks. Finish the jelly cake by spreading a tart jelly, such as red currant or wild plum between the layers. Allow to set up for 1/2 hour before serving.

SEPTEMBER 15, 1883

Since the passage of the 1862 Homestead law and up to June 30, 1883, the total number of homestead entries numbered 608,632. Last year the entries numbered 3,146. The Land Office at Washington is now preparing what will be by far the most interesting statement it has ever published. It will show the total amount of public land disposed of from the first and will afford the means of calculating, for the first time with any degree of accuracy, how much of the public domain remains.

Rolled Jelly Cake

1 cup sugar
4 eggs, separated
1 cup flour
1 teaspoon baking powder

Preheat the oven to 375 degrees F. Beat the egg yolks and sugar until thick and lemon colored. Whip the egg whites with grease-free beaters in a clean bowl until stiff peaks form. Sift the flour and baking powder. Fold the flour into the egg and sugar mixture. Fold in the egg whites. Grease a jelly roll pan and line with a sheet of parchment or waxed paper. Grease the parchment. Pour the batter in and spread evenly. Bake until cake is firm and lightly browned, 15 to 20 minutes. Spread with jelly as soon as it is baked, roll the cake up. Cool and serve.

APRIL 4, 1885

Feather Cake

Bake feather cake in a loaf, or the next time in layers, and put jelly between. Again, make it with the whites of two eggs using the yolks for custard flavored with orange or lemon, to put between the layers. Next time make a chocolate filling and I venture to say your men folks will never suspect you are giving them the same kind of cake all the time and one so inexpensive, too. — Mrs. E.B.T.

1 cup sugar
1 tablespoon butter
1 egg
2/3 cup milk
2 teaspoons baking powder
2 1/2 cups flour

Preheat the oven to 350 degrees F. Sift the flour and baking powder. Cream together the sugar, butter and egg. Add half the flour mixture, the milk and the rest of the flour. Pour into greased and floured pan and bake until lightly browned. Baking time: 45 minutes for loaf and 30 minutes for layers.

Note: Most of the 19th-century chocolate and other cake fillings use uncooked eggs or egg whites, a risky practice. I suggest filling the cakes with a cooked custard or regular chocolate butter cream frosting.

Simple Breakfast Cake

This cake can be very quickly made and is much less trouble than muffins or gems. —Mrs. Sears

2 cups flour
2 teaspoons baking powder
1 egg
1 cup half and half

Preheat the oven to 375 degrees F. Sift together the flour and baking powder and put into a medium mixing bowl. Combine the egg and the half and half. Stir into the flour and pour into a lightly greased cake pan. Bake until lightly browned and firm in the center, 20 to 25 minutes. Serve warm with butter.

OCTOBER 20, 1888

Lemon Loaf Cake

I never throw away the refuse lemon halves left after cake making or after lemonade. They will be found to have very useful properties. The cook can clean her hands with them or she will find them useful for taking stains from her platters and sauce pans.

—Mrs. Hart

1 cup butter
3 cups sugar
5 egg yolks
1/2 teaspoon baking soda
1 cup milk
4 cups flour
Juice and rind of one lemon
5 beaten egg whites

Preheat the oven to 350 degrees F. Cream the butter and sugar. Stir in the egg yolks and beat well. Stir in the baking soda and two cups flour. Add the milk and then the remaining flour. Stir in the lemon juice and rind. Fold in the beaten egg whites. Grease and flour three 4- by 8-inch loaf pans. Divide the batter among them. Bake until cake is firm in the center and slightly pulled away from the sides, about 45 minutes.

Coffee Cake

1 cup firmly packed brown sugar
1 1/2 cup butter
2 eggs
1 cup molasses
1 cup cold coffee
3 cups flour
1 teaspoon soda
1 teaspoon cream of tartar
1 teaspoon cinnamon
1 teaspoon cloves
1 teaspoon allspice
1/2 teaspoon nutmeg
1/2 pound raisins
1/4 pound citron

Preheat the oven to 350 degrees F. Cream the butter and sugar. Add the eggs and molasses and beat well. Combine the flour, cream of tartar, baking soda and spices. Take out 1/2 cup and mix with the raisins and citron. Set aside. Add half the flour mixture to the creamed ingredients, then the coffee and lastly the rest of the flour, mixing well after each addition. Stir in the flour-dredged fruit. Grease and flour two 8- or 9-inch square pans. Divide the batter between them. Bake until the cake is firm in the center and a tester comes out clean, about 1 hour.

Cottage Cheese Cheesecake

24 ounces 1% (fat) cottage cheese
3 eggs, separated
4 tablespoons melted butter
1/3 cup flour
3/4 cup sugar
3/4 cup nonfat sour cream
1 1/2 teaspoons grated lemon peel
1/4 cup lemon juice
1/4 teaspoon nutmeg

1 graham cracker crumb crust
in spring-form pan
or 2 "ready made" crusts in pie pans

Topping, optional
1 egg
3/4 cup nonfat sour cream
1/2 cup sugar

Preheat the oven to 325 degrees F. Drain the cottage cheese while you make and bake the crust. Put the cheese, eggs, melted butter, flour, sugar, 3/4 cup sour cream, nutmeg, lemon peel and juice in a blender or food processor and blend until mixture is smooth. Pour into cool, prepared crust. Bake until firm in the center about 1 hour to 1 1/4 hours. Cool the cheesecake. Mix the topping ingredients. Pour over cooled cheesecake and bake for 10 minutes. Cool cheesecake over night, or at least 4 hours before serving. Store in refrigerator.

Fruit Cake

I always select a day to bake my fruitcakes for Thanksgiving and Christmas when the stove will not be wanted for anything else and I can regulate the fire to suit my baking. The recipe is one I have had for a long time, in fact the fruit cake for my wedding was made from it.

—*Mrs. Knox*

1 dozen eggs
1 pound sugar
1 pound butter
1 pound flour
1 tablespoon each cinnamon, mace and nutmeg
1/2 cup milk
2 pounds each raisins and currants
1 pounds citron

Preheat the oven to 325 degrees F. Beat egg whites until stiff and set aside. Cream the butter and sugar. Add the egg yolks and beat well. Combine the flour and spices and set aside 1/2 cup to mix with the fruits. Stir in half the flour, next the milk and then the rest of the flour, beating well after each addition. Stir in the flour-dredged fruit. Carefully fold in the stiffly beaten egg whites. Turn the batter into two well-greased and floured loaf pans. Bake 1 to 1 1/2 hours or until the cake is firm and slightly pulled away from the sides.

Note: For a more moist cake, bake the loaves in a water bath by putting the loaf pans in a larger pan filled halfway up the sides with boiling water.

August 18, 1883

Little Sam Wrinkler on visiting a neighboring family last Saturday was addressed by the lady of the house: "What can I do for you, my little man?" she asked.

"I dunno," said Sam.

"Mamma told me not to ask for cake or pie, as I did last time, and I'm sorter at a loss to know what to ask for, for I don't know what else ye've got in yer pantry, anyhow; but I can put up with most anything that's handy."

Plainer Fruit Cake

1 package dried apples (5 ounces)
(Chop as small as currants.)
2 cups molasses
1 cup sugar
1/2 cup shortening (butter or margarine)
"Beef drippings answer very well."
3 egg yolks or the whole of 2 eggs
1 cup sour cream
Spice to taste:
1 1/2 teaspoons cinnamon
1 teaspoon nutmeg
1/2 teaspoon cloves
1 teaspoon soda
4 1/2 cups flour
1 cup raisins

With kitchen scissors or in a food processor, cut the dried apples into very small pieces, about the size of currants. Soak them in water over night. In the morning, drain them well and pat dry. Combine with the molasses and simmer until the apples are very tender, about 1/2 hour. (You could do this step in a microwave.) Preheat the oven to 325 degrees F. Cream the shortening and sugar. Stir in the eggs. Combine the flour with the baking soda and spices. Add half the flour, the sour cream and the remaining flour. Stir in the apple/molasses mixture and the raisins. Pour batter into a large, well-greased and floured angel food cake pan. Fill about two-thirds full. Bake 1 1/4 hours or until the cake is firm in the center and pulled away slightly from the sides.

Note: The original recipe says only to "soak the apples" overnight. I have suggested water, but certainly one could use brandy or cider to give more flavor to the cake.

January 6, 1859
An ill-timed prayer: Last summer at Mill, a messenger having requested a London clergyman to announce "If Dr. Smith is among the audience, he is urgently wanted," the clergyman added from sympathy, "and may God have mercy on the poor patient." The doctor, in a rage, demanded and received an apology.

CHAPTER NINE

Pies

Pies are at once one of the easiest and the most confusing categories in 19th century cooking. The pioneer diaries frequently mention pie baking. How hard can it be to make a simple short crust, throw in the fruit and put it in the oven? Yet, cookbooks of the era, and even articles in *Prairie Farmer,* decry pie as being indigestible and unhealthful. The recipes either have way too much filling or seemingly not enough. In short, it is not as easy as pie.

But the recipes in *Prairie Farmer* are unusual and well worth the effort of figuring out how to make them in today's kitchens. The Lemon Cream Pie is a case in point. I must have made this pie 10 times before I achieved one worthy of Clara Frances' comment, "We think there is no dessert equal to this pie." The original measurements needed to be decoded from "Tablespoon" and "Large Tablespoon." I needed to realize the

> *"If as a nation we were less devoted to the inevitable 'pie' we would not be, as we are, a nation of dyspeptics."*
> **April 28, 1877**
>
> *"There is nothing that goes right to the spot like a generous slice of pie."*
> **November 23, 1876**

filling went right into the crust without pre-cooking. And, as 6- or 7-inch pie tins are not commonly available, as they were in 1871, I needed to find the right size in which to bake it. The filling works very nicely in a commonly purchased 8-inch graham cracker crust and is, indeed, a wonderful pie.

Let me comment on complaints of the unhealthfulness of pies in the 1800s. One clue presents itself in period cookbooks. Many of them call for baking pies in puff pastry, like the frozen turnovers we buy today. While it may work for turnovers, where there is a small amount of filling for the flaky layers to surround, in a pie tin, it is quite a different matter. The top crust may work fine, but the under crust is a soggy, and yes, indigestible, mess. Fortunately the writers in *Prairie Farmer* most often recommended the common short crust, making for a much better, and digestible, product.

Beet Pie

Editor's Note:

These three pieces about beet pies illustrate just how vibrant the dialogue could be between *Prairie Farmer* subscribers and editors.

The red beet generally appears on our tables in acid and cold forms as a pickle only; whereas, if our female friends would take the matter in hand, we doubt not that it could be prepared in a variety of ways, superior to any garden production which we possess — as it is abundantly and easily cultivated, and kept in a state of perfect freshness during the whole year. By a recent trial, it has been found that pies may be made of it, which are equal to if not superior to rhubarb — either from the leaves, the same as rhubarb, or from the root — by cutting it into square pieces. Vinegar and sugar and other spices if liked, can be added to suit any palate. It possesses the advantage of furnishing us with a delicate and beautiful pie which can grace our tables at any season of the year.

Beet Pie Continued

Noticing recently in a Philadelphia paper, a statement that the beet makes a palatable pie, I pared and grated two beets to a pulp with which my daughter made pies, which in quality and relish would not fall behind many that are made from more costly materials, especially to us in the West. Let the beet be pared and grated fine on a common tin grater, or scraped with a knife; then stir into it about half a gill of good vinegar to a pint of pulp. Sweeten and spice to your taste, and bake it thoroughly. Try it.

—J.T. Gifford

Sally, in the Maine Farmer, complains most bitterly of imposition in being induced to make beet pies, which "neither man, cat, dog, nor cow could eat with any kind of grace; not even a hog, unless very hungry, and then at long intervals of severe squealing." Suppose she should try Mr. Gifford's recipe. Mr. Holmes, the editor, treats the case good-naturedly, and asks a serious question: Wouldn't the pie be as good accompaniment for the sawdust puddings that we editors are glad to get?

—Prairie Farmer editor

Song of the Pumpkin

Written on receive the gift of a Pumpkin Pie, By A. Yankee

Oh! Queenly and fair in the lands of the sun,
The vines of the gourd and rich melon run,
And the rock and the tree and the cottage enfold,
With broad leaves all greenness and blossoms all gold.
Like that which o'er Ninevah's prophet once grew,
While he waited to know that his warning was true,
And longed for the storm-cloud, and listened in vain
For the rush of the whirlwind and red fire-rain.

On the banks of the Xenil the dark Spanish maiden
Comes up with the fruit of the tangled vine laden;
And the Creole of Cuba laughs out to behold
Through orange leaves shining the broad spheres of gold;
Yet with the dearer delight from his home in the North
On the fields of his harvest the Yankee looks forth
Where the crook-necks are coiling and yellow fruit shines
And the sun of September beams down on his vines.

Ah! On Thanksgiving Day when from East and from West,
From North and from South come the pilgrim and guest
When the gray-haired New Englander sees round his board
The old broken links of affection restored,
When the care-wearied man seeks his mother once more
And the worn matron smiles where the girl smiled before,
What moistens the lip and what brightens the eye?
What calls back the past, like the rich Pumpkin Pie?

Oh! Fruit loved of boyhood, the old days recalling,
When wood-grapes were purpling and brown nuts were falling!
When wild, ugly faces were carved in its skin.
Glaring out through the dark with a candle within!
When we laughed round the corn heap, with hearts all in tune,
Our chair a broad pumpkin — our lantern the moon,
Telling tails of the fairy who travels like steam,
In a pumpkin-shell coach, with two rats for her team!

Then thanks for thy present — none sweeter or better
E'er smoked from an oven or circled a platter!
Fair hands ne'er wrought a pastry more fine,
Brighter eyes ne'er watched o'er its baking than thine!
And the prayer which my mouth is too full to express
Swells my heart that thy shadow may never be less;
That the days of thy worth like a pumpkin vine grow,
And thy life be as sweet, and its last sunset sky,
Golden-tinted and fair as thy own Pumpkin Pie!

A PRAIRIE Kitchen

Pumpkin Pie

The almost universal mode in New England of preparing pumpkin for pies (a kind that is universally admired) is that of stewing the pumpkin after it has been cut in pieces and passing it through one of two other processes before it is in a state for baking — thereby making much labor. I think a more preferable mode of preparation, and one which I believe will be highly valued by all housewives, is that of grating the pumpkin; after grating add the milk, eggs &c., in the same proportions as usual. Your domestic readers will find that pies made this way are equally nice and even more delicate with one-third the labor.
—*The North Hampton Courier*

November 1852
Rub lard on pie plate. Sprinkle with dry corn meal. Put in prepared pumpkin. "Bake quick and you will have a nice pie."

Cheap Pie

Editor's note:

If you like molasses, you will like this pie. It really is more like a glazed crust, as the filling is quite thin. But it is a rich pie and very satisfying, especially with a bit of ice cream on the side.

Crust for a two-crust pie
1/4 cup molasses
2 tablespoons flour
1/2 teaspoon cinnamon

Preheat the oven to 350 degrees F. Combine the molasses, flour and cinnamon. Spread it over the bottom crust. Top with the second crust and roll the edges together. You will end up with a very flat pie with a thick outer edge, sort of like a pizza with a top crust. Cut small slits in the top crust to vent any steam. Bake until the crust is light brown, about 25 to 30 minutes. The molasses mixture may bubble out of the slits.

Minced Pie

Equally as good as pie made with apples, and in a scarcity of fruit, is well worth trying.

3/4 pound cooked beef, homemade boiled is best, but roast from the deli will work
2 jars sliced pickled beets
1 teaspoon cinnamon
1 teaspoon mace
1/2 teaspoon cloves
1/3 cup molasses
1/3 cup vinegar
1 cup raisins
1 cup currents
1/2 cup brown sugar
Hot water to make the mass of a proper consistency, if necessary
1 teaspoon butter to each pie

Put the beef and beets in the food processor or grinder and chop until about the size of the currants. Combine all the ingredients in a microwave-safe bowl. Cover with a lid or plastic wrap. Cook at 1/2 power for 5 minutes; stir and cook for another 5 minutes. Set aside in the refrigerator overnight to mellow. Use as you would regular mincemeat in pies or tarts.

Vinegar Pie

August 25, 1883
Aunt Esther was trying to persuade little Edy to retire at sunset, using as an argument that the little chickens went to roost at that time. "Yes," said Edy, "but then, Aunty, the old hen always goes with them."

1 cup water
1 cup sharp vinegar
3 cups sorghum
1/3 cup grated cracker crumbs or soda biscuit
1/2 cup butter
1 teaspoon nutmeg or 2 teaspoons lemon extract

Prepare standard crust for a two-crust pie. Preheat the oven to 350 degrees F. Combine the water, vinegar and sorghum and boil, stirring for 5 minutes. Stir in the cracker crumbs and butter. Add the flavoring. Put into the pie crust and bake for 35 minutes or until the crust is golden.

Pie Plant Pie (Rhubarb)

Crust for a two-crust pie, 8-inch
2 cups rhubarb
(sliced in 1/4-inch or smaller slices)
2 cups boiling water
2 tablespoons butter
2 tablespoons flour
1/2 teaspoon nutmeg
3 or 4 tablespoons sorghum

Editor's note:

This is a real pioneer pie, using two of the most readily available prairie ingredients — rhubarb and sorghum. Rhubarb has commonly been called "pie plant" since colonial days. By blanching the rhubarb, you remove some of the bitterness, so you need less sweetening. If you don't care for the taste of sorghum or molasses, you might try making it with corn syrup.

Put the thinly sliced rhubarb in a heatproof container and pour the boiling water over it. Let it stand until the water is cold, 20 minutes or so. Preheat the oven to 425 degrees F. Drain off the rhubarb water. (You may reserve it to make Rhubarb Lemonade by combining with 1/4 cup lemon juice and sugar to taste.) Pat the rhubarb dry and place in pie pan lined with the bottom crust. Dust with flour and nutmeg, and dot with butter. Drizzle the sorghum over the top evenly. Top with upper crust, sealing the edges and cutting slits for the juices to vent. Bake for 15 minutes at 425 degrees F., then lower the oven to 350 degrees F. and continue baking until the crust is golden and the juices have begun to bubble, about 30 minutes longer.

Rhubarb Pie Plant

In new counties and on new farms where fruit is scarce, there is nothing else that can so nearly take its place as the stalks of the rhubarb plant. If good roots are set out, it often yields quite well even the first year, as I proved by experience last season. And the second spring it will be just in its prime.

It requires a good deal of sugar when cooked,

as it is so strongly acid, but as that is the only expense incurred by its use, it is not extravagant, especially in these days when sugar is so cheap. It comes so early in the spring before any fresh fruit is to be had, except at exorbitant prices for that which is shipped from the South or California. A moderate use of it cooked in different ways, is really healthful, I think.

—Mrs. Emma T. King

Emergency Pie

Sometimes we are without fruit and something is needed to complete the dinner. I have a recipe for a pie that the children have named "emergency pie" from my having to use it on such occasions. I find, however, every person likes it.
—Mrs. Harris

Editor's note:

The original recipe does not specify a flavoring. However, a teaspoon of cinnamon or the grated rind and juice of a lemon are good additions.

1 bottom crust for an 8-inch pie
1 cup flour
1/4 cup sugar
3/4 cup melted butter
2 eggs

Preheat oven to 325 degrees F. Combine the flour and sugar and add the melted butter. Stir in the eggs and mix well. Pour into the pie crust and bake until the filling is firm, about 35 minutes.

Peach Pie

A very popular dessert with us is peach pie. Of course good, sweet well-ripened fruit is necessary to success. Peel, cut in halves and lay as closely as possible over the crust in a deep pie plate, with the open part upwards. Sprinkle with sugar to taste. Then beat well together a large teacup full of milk, 2 tablespoons sugar, one egg, a little vanilla and a pinch of salt and pour this over the peaches and bake without any upper crust. Eat when partly cool. Canned peaches can be thus used quite well when fresh ones are out of season.
—Mrs. Norse

Lemon Pie with Raisins

Having being very much given to pie-eat-y from early youth, I trust I may be forgiven for presenting the readers of the Farmer, a few suggestions in regard to this department of cookery. I will commence with lemon pies. For those decoctions of lemons, grated crackers, eggs and what not, which are denominated lemon pies, I wouldn't give a fig! The only genuine way in which to make this peer of pies is with lemons, raisins and molasses.

Owing to the costliness of these pies, as well as their being not strictly an article of healthy diet, it is expected that they will not be indulged in except on holidays — besides their deliciousness might breed a contempt for commoner foods.
—Marie Mignonette

Crust for one 10-inch, two-crust pie,
or two 7-inch, two-crust pies
2 cups golden raisins
2 lemons, juice and rind
2 cups molasses

Preheat the oven to 425 degrees F. Combine the filling ingredients in a medium saucepan and cook for 5 minutes. Set aside to cool. You will need three layers from your pie crust — the bottom and top and a very thin layer in the middle of the pie. I know it sounds strange, but it somehow works to thicken the filling and cut the sweetness. So divide your pie crust into uneven thirds; the part for the center is smaller than for the bottom or the top crusts. Roll the bottom and top crust a bit thinner than usual. The center crust is as thin as you can make it. Put the bottom crust in the pie tin; fill with half the filling. Put in the center crust and the rest of the filling. Top with the upper crust. Seal the edge well and cut slits for the steam to escape. Bake 15 minutes, then lower the heat to 350 and continue baking until the crust is golden and the filling is bubbly, about another 30 minutes.

Lemon Cream Pie

We think that there is no dessert equal to this pie. —Clara Francis

Crust for one 8-inch pie
3/4 cup sugar
1/2 cup flour
2 tablespoons butter, very soft
1 cup milk
3 egg yolks
Juice and grated rind of one lemon

Preheat the oven to 350 degrees F. Combine the flour and sugar in a medium mixing bowl. Add the butter, milk and egg yolks, mixing well. Finally, stir in the lemon juice and rind. Pour into the pie shell, bake until the filling is softly set, about 40 minutes. If you test with a knife, a bit of the filling will stick, but it will be like pudding, not runny. The filling thickens as the pie cools. Store in the refrigerator. If you use an 8-inch crust, there is room for whipped cream on top.

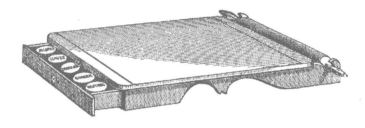

OCTOBER 3, 1885

Green Tomato Pie

Take medium-sized tomatoes, pare and cut out the stem ends. Having your pie plate lined with a paste made of biscuit dough, slice the tomatoes very thin, filling the pan somewhat heaping. Then grate over it half a nutmeg. Put in half a cup of butter and a medium cup of sugar.

Sprinkle a small handful of flour over all, pouring in half a cup of water before adding the top crust. Bake half an hour in a moderately hot oven, serving hot. Is good, try it.
—Mrs. Louise Harris, Bond County, Ill.

CHAPTER TEN

Beverages

What did settlers drink on the prairie? Early diaries suggest that water and tea were the mainstays in the home, along with the more expensive coffee. As the land became more settled, innkeepers in town offered beers, wines and stronger drink from out East. But in the country, farmers relied on a variety of homemade specialties.

> *"Although we would discountenance the daily use of alcohol in any shape, we give, among other receipts, directions for the concocting of drinks containing it, because of their medicinal qualities and the extreme benefit to be derived from them by persons suffering from general debility."*
> July 7, 1877

century. *Prairie Farmer* columnists expressed concern for "tippling," drinking alcoholic beverages to excess, and the writers included fruit-flavored vinegars to keep their husbands and farm workers away from stronger drink. Diluted alcoholic drinks did appear in the magazine pages, however. Although the inclusion of the Blackberry Cordial with a pint of brandy as a tonic for children does seem contrary to the temperance ideal.

From ginger beer to haymaker's drink, the recipes in this chapter demonstrate the enjoyment prairie farmers took in specially prepared beverages to refresh, cool and invigorate. These recipes provide the same enjoyment today. There is no finer summer drink than the easily made ginger lemonade — sweet, tart and soothing with the inclusion of fresh ginger root, recognized in the 19th century as a tonic.

The temperance movement was quite strong all over the United States during the second half of the 19th

The last two pages in this chapter provide a special window into farm life during the 1880s, reflecting the opposite influences of tradition and sophistication. Haymaker's Drink draws upon years of experience for a good, almost nourishing, beverage to keep the workers healthy in the hot fields during harvest. The letter inquiring about cocoa underscores the increasing availability of foods from east and west coasts and even overseas to farmers in the heartland.

Cooling Drinks for Summer

When the intense warmth of the sun makes the blood seethe in our veins, we crave a beverage which will quench our thirst without adding warmth to the system; and if we resort to iced but intoxicating liquors they will surely inflame it and increase instead of decreasing the desire for liquids. A great quantity of iced water is also undesirable, because it will chill the stomach too suddenly, and often produce complaints to which we are liable at this season. But the appetite craves some agreeable aromatic stimulant, and there is no beverage more healthful than ginger beer, while there are few more refreshing; and it is easily prepared in dry powders or in liquid form.

—Clara Francis

Ginger Beer Powders

These are made by taking to every 4 ounces of powdered white sugar, 1 drachm of pulverized ginger and 5 drachms of carbonate of soda. Divide it into 12 equal parts and do up each portion in a colored paper. Then take 1 ounce of tartaric acid, divide it into 12 parts and do up each portion in a white paper. Dissolve one of each kind of powders into a third of a tumbler of iced water; stir it until it is all dissolved, but the ginger, then pour one into the other and drink while effervescing.

Claret Cup

This makes a pleasant drink for picnics and garden parties, but unless the claret is good it cannot be well flavored. Mix in a large pitcher. To one bottle of claret add 4 tablespoons sugar, 2 or 3 slices of lemon, 1 thin slice down the length of a cucumber and 1/4 teaspoon nutmeg. Let it stand after stirring it up thoroughly for a quarter of an hour and then taste it.

If the lemon and cucumber flavors are decided, take them out. Now add a quantity of ice in rather large pieces and then pour in a pint bottle of soda-water, taking care to turn it in with the neck of the bottle close to the claret so as not to lose the effervescence. Serve at once.

Strawberry Sherbet

1 quart strawberries
6 cups water
Juice of 1 lemon
1 1/2 cups sugar

Editor's note:

This is a wonderfully simple concoction. In the 1870s, sherbet referred to a beverage. A very similar recipe appears in 1888, but the final directions include freezing in an ice cream freezer. Ice cream has been made in the United States since the early 1800s, so it may be an indication of the scarcity of ice that has this served as a beverage.

Mash the strawberries, or put them through a food processor. Mix with the lemon juice and water, set aside for 3 hours. Drain the juice though a fine sieve and discard the solids. Add the sugar and mix until it is dissolved. Set aside in the freezer for 2 or 3 hours, or simply pour over ice.

Lemonade

Allow 3 or 4 lemons according to size and juiciness to each quart of water and about 2 tablespoons of sugar to each lemon. Roll the lemons until soft, then slice them upon the sugar and mix well, pressing the lemon to extract the juice.

Add a little water and let stand for 20 minutes. Add the remainder of the water, ice well, stir thoroughly and pour out. Oranges substituted for a portion of the lemons give a delightful flavor; in this case lessen the quantity of sugar.

JULY 7, 1877

Sherbet: It's Good

In the glowing heat of a July day, we seat ourselves for our weekly chat with the readers of the Prairie Farmer. In vain we cudgel our brains for a topic of interest. Life has one chief aim. Minor matters are effectually overshadowed by the all-absorbing question: how to keep cool. Out of the abundance of the heart, the mouth speaketh, and our limp energies are roused into activity by contemplating the pleasing topic of cooling beverages.

—*Clara Francis*

Blackberry Cordial

Editor's note:

I certainly would never give this to a child, but sipped from small glasses by ladies after dinner it is an elegant drink. You can also leave out the alcohol and mix this with still or sparkling water for a more refreshing summer beverage.

Mix together 1 quart blackberry juice, 1 pound sugar, a spice bag of 1 teaspoon cloves, 1 teaspoon allspice, 2 teaspoons cinnamon, 2 teaspoons nutmeg and 1 pint good brandy. This is a most excellent remedy to be given to children for the complaints to which they are subject during the summer months, the dose being one half a tablespoonful as occasion may require.

—Clara Francis

JULY 7, 1877

Milk Punch

Beat an egg very light with sugar. Add it to a couple of tablespoonful of good brandy, stir well, and finally add a glass of rich milk. Or the egg can be omitted using only brandy, sugar and milk. Ice well before giving to the patient. Persons unable to eat food can be kept alive for days upon this mixture.

—Clara Francis

April 7, 1866
Preparing Coffee
Brown evenly, but not too dark, one pound of coffee; as soon as done, while hot, add sufficient brown sugar to make the coffee look glistening. Grind as wanted. Boiling spoils coffee as well as tea, all of the delicate aroma going off in the steam.

Ginger Lemonade

Editor's note:

Here are two versions of ginger lemonade as they appeared in *Prairie Farmer*. If you aren't up to the task, skip to my adapted recipe below.

This is a pleasant drink in hot weather and not particularly tedious to make. Boil 6 1/2 pounds of loaf sugar for five minutes in 5 gallons of water. Clear it with the whites of 3 eggs. Bruise a quarter of a pound of common ginger. Boil with the liquor and then pour it over 5 lemons, pared. When cold, put it in a cask with 1 tablespoon of yeast. Bung up the cask the next day and it will be ready to use in two weeks.

—Mrs. Dow

It was so very warm last week and the men who were working very hard complained of feeling the ill effects of drinking so much water. I made a drink for them after a recipe of my mother's. Put 2 gallons of cold water into a kettle on to heat. Add to it 2 ounces of good ginger and 2 ounces of white or brown sugar. Let it all come to a boil and continue boiling for one hour. Then skim the liquid and put it into a tub with 1 sliced lemon and 1/2 ounce of cream of tartar. When nearly cold, put in 1 teaspoonful of yeast to cause the liquor to work. After several days, strain and bottle, and it is ready for use.

—Mrs. Owen

Adapted Ginger Lemonade

Make a simple syrup of
1 cup sugar
1 cup water
Fresh ginger root,
2 inches long and 1 inch in diameter
2 lemons

Simmer until the sugar is dissolved. Add peeled ginger root, cut into thin slices. Peel the rind from the lemons in strips and add to the simmering syrup. Cook for 10 minutes or until the ginger root and lemon peel appear transparent. Strain the syrup into a heat-proof container. When it is cool stir in the juice from the lemons.

To serve: Pour 1/4 cup syrup into a glass, stir in 2/3 to 3/4 cup sparkling water and ice. Keep unused syrup in the refrigerator for up to a week.

Raspberry Vinegar

1 quart fresh raspberries
(or two 12-ounce packages
frozen raspberries)
1 cup white vinegar
2 cups sugar (or more)

Editor's note:

Raspberry vinegar and other fruit, vinegar and sugar beverages have been served in America since colonial days. Frequently called "shrubs," they are a predecessor to our common lemonade. In a typically Midwestern variation (I have a recipe from the June 1837 issue of *Tennessee Farmer*), the cook cuts up stalks from the ubiquitous rhubarb plant and mixes them with sugar to begin extracting the juice. If you try this option, let it stand overnight, bring to a simmer and cook until the rhubarb is tender and then strain the juice through a jelly bag. You can then add some lemon or orange juice to the syrup and mix with water. This is a very pretty delicate pink. Even rhubarb haters, will enjoy this beverage.

Put raspberries in glass jar with vinegar. Let the jar stand in a cool place, such as the cellar or refrigerator, two or three days, giving it an occasional shake. Mash berries and strain through cheesecloth or jelly bag. Measure the juice and pour into a heavy saucepan. Stir in twice as much sugar as there is juice. Bring to a boil slowly. Reduce heat and simmer, stirring occasionally, for 20 minutes. Pour the syrup into jars and keep in the refrigerator for a week. The syrup may also be frozen.

To serve: Mix 1 or 2 tablespoons to a glass of water or soda and serve over ice.

Chocolate and Cocoa

A reader of the Prairie Farmer asks where chocolate is raised? Chocolate and cocoa are similar preparations being made from the pods, seeds, etc. of a tropical palm tree which is very abundant in the West Indies, especially the Caribbean Islands. The chocolate is made by roasting the pods like coffee, and making it into a paste, either with or without sugar.

It is sometimes flavored with vanilla. "French chocolate" was long thought to be unrivaled, but that now extensively prepared in this country is by many persons thought to be superior to the French. The shells or husks removed from the beans make a weaker preparation, which is much used, especially by invalids and children.

An Old Fashioned Tea

Having become much interested in the reports of the Housekeepers' Improvement Club, I send an item to the secretary as my contribution to the talks. Can there be, after all, any improvement upon our old-fashioned "tea" of 40 years ago, as we had them when I was home on the farm? We could get up a "tea" or supper to suit the occasion on very short notice. If we were surprised by company driving up through our grove of native oaks, we were always ready with a hearty welcome to receive them, and our tea would be quickly made ready, new and fresh.

Mother would throw out some bread crumbs near the back door and a few scattering ones inside, to attract the chickens; and after the first crumbs were devoured, they would come to the near ones, and just at the nick of time the door was closed and the chickens imprisoned. Then mother would get her eye on a good nice one and catch it. Hot water from the teakettle and nimble hands soon removed the feathers, when it was speedily cut up and put into the pot. The table, spread with snowy white linen and set with old-fashioned gold-banded china, was a welcome sight. With chicken, we would have saleratus bis-cuit, made with a pint of sour cream and a few spoonfuls of butter, rolled thin and baked in a hot oven. In the meantime, three or four fresh eggs were beaten and a steamed custard preceded, using plenty of the morning's cream to make it rich.

We always kept on hand a stock of cake such as pound, fruit, and jelly cake and a few slices of each would make an ample showing. Then from the cellar came a glass dish filled with preserved quinces or peaches. With these dainties on the table, and chicken stewed to perfection, with the gravy properly seasoned and thickened, a few bis-cuits split one and laid on the platter underneath, the gravy poured over it, and a smoking hot cup of tea, we had a repast that all enjoyed. Guests and family seated around such a table would now call it old-fashioned indeed, but I would not care to improve upon the old style, were I a member of the Housekeepers' Improvement Club and living on a farm.
—Mrs. A.E.H., Milwaukee, Wis.

Haymaker's Drink

When Mr. Burns comes time for haying, I always take rye or barley and brown it just right for coffee and then add one-third as much sweet corn without burning. Then I grind it together and make as much coffee as I think will be drunk in harvest during the day. I do not make it very strong or sweet. I strain off into a jug, which they keep in the shade. Mr. Burns says he considers it the best and healthiest drink for harvest he ever tried. It is very sustaining and the men seldom care much for lunch who are using it.
—Mrs. Burns

STEAMING BREAD IN THE MICROWAVE

I have used the microwave to steam breads, cakes and puddings instead of boiling them on top of the stove. You need a microwaveable container that is generally in the shape of a loaf of bread standing on its end. A plastic 2-pound yogurt carton or an 8-inch-tall by 4-inch-wide square microwave serving/ storage container work well. You also need waxed paper, kitchen string and a sharp pointed implement like a bamboo skewer or Phillips-head screwdriver.

Fill the container about two-thirds full with the batter. Cover the top with four thickness of waxed paper. Tie the waxed paper firmly around the container using kitchen string. Punch holes through the paper about an inch apart in all directions. Put the container into the microwave and begin "steaming" at half power for five minutes. Repeat as necessary until the loaf is firm and just begins to pull away from the side. If you over cook the loaf, it will become tough. Because the power of microwave ovens varies, some experimenting will be needed to determine the exact timing and power setting for your oven. The results are well worth the effort. I have made six loaves of Boston Brown Bread in less than 30 minutes. The old-fashioned method would have taken at least two hours and steamed up the kitchen as well.

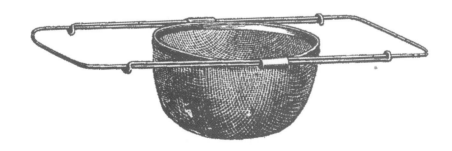

INDEX

V

W

Articles

Ordering Cookbooks

"A Prairie Kitchen" cookbook is a cooking asset for your kitchen and a great gift for any cookbook collector, history buff, antique collector, or anyone interested in expanding their recipe selection. This cookbook gives you unlimited inspiration to plan menus or prepare special treats with authentic historical flare.

Additionally, the stories and snippets excerpted from the pages of *Prairie Farmer* magazine editions published from 1841 to 1900 present you with historical vignettes and authentic prairie culture and perspectives.

"A Prairie Kitchen" is more than a cookbook, it's a profile of America's proud pioneer spirit.

Cookbooks may be ordered from the publisher. Please contact us for pricing. Bulk discounts are available.

> **By Mail:**
> Farm Progress Companies
> 191 South Gary Avenue
> Carol Stream, IL 60188
>
> **By Telephone:**
> (800) 441-1410
> or
> (630) 690-5600
>
> **By E-Mail:**
> *sales@farmprogress.com*

Additional cookbook information may be obtained from our Web address:
> *www.farmprogress.com*